Don McCullin's photogst thirty years, provided pog testimony to man's inhumanity to man. But at what cost to the eyes behind the lens?

DON McCULLIN
Unreasonable Behaviour
AN AUTOBIOGRAPHY

Beginning with childhood poverty and teenage gang warfare in North London, McCullin recounts his first attempts at finding a bridge between the two worlds of Fleet Street and the biking bombers of Finsbury Park. After his baptism by fire in Cyprus, he faces the horrors of mercenary battles in the jungles of the Congo and, worse, of Vietnam at Hue and during the Tet offensive. He is profoundly shocked by his first encounter with the plight of starving children caught in the Biafran struggle. He is wounded by the Khmer Rouge in Cambodia. He describes his attempts to save Nick Tomalin when his car is hit on the Golan Heights, his narrow escape from Pol Pot, a brush with warlike mullahs in Iran, adventures with Roger Cooper in Afghanistan, investigating genocide in Latin America with Norman Lewis, more painful damage in El Salvador and the shattering experience of recording the wholesale murder of civilians in Beirut.

UNREASONABLE BEHAVIOUR is the story of a man adrift in a personal wilderness, witness to the unimaginable.

Illustrated with 48 pages of plates, featuring over 70 of McCullin's own photographs — many published for the first time.

Jonathan Cape • October 18 • £15.95 • ISBN 0 224 02655 0

WHAT WENT WRONG?

33

Editor: Bill Buford
Commissioning Editor: Lucretia Stewart
Assistant Editor: Tim Adams
Managing Editor: Angus MacKinnon
Assistant to the Editor: Ursula Doyle

Managing Director: Caroline Michel
Circulation Director: Sarah Bristow
Financial Controller: Michael Helm
Publishing Assistant: Sally Lewis
Subscriptions: Carol Harris
Office Assistant: Stephen Taylor

Picture Editor: Alice Rose George
Picture Research: Sally Lewis
Design: Chris Hyde
Executive Editor: Pete de Bolla
US Associate Publisher: Anne Kinard, Granta, 250 West 57th Street,
Suite 1316, New York, NY 10107.

Editorial and Subscription Correspondence: Granta, 2-3 Hanover
Yard, Noel Road, Islington, London N1 8BE. Telephone: (071) 704
9776. Fax: (071) 704 0474. Subscriptions: (071) 704 0470.
A one-year subscription (four issues) is £19.95 in Britain, £25.95 for
the rest of Europe and £31.95 for the rest of the world.
All manuscripts are welcome but must be accompanied by a
stamped, self-addressed envelope or they cannot be returned.

Granta is printed by BPCC Hazell Books Ltd, Aylesbury, Bucks.

Granta is published by Granta Publications Ltd and distributed by
Penguin Books Ltd, Harmondsworth, Middlesex, England; Viking
Penguin, a division of Penguin Books USA Inc, 375 Hudson Street,
New York, NY 10014, USA; Penguin Books Australia Ltd,
Ringwood, Victoria, Australia; Penguin Books Canada Ltd, 2801
John Street, Markham, Ontario, Canada L3R 1BR; Penguin Books
(NZ) Ltd, 182-190 Wairau Road, Auckland 10, New Zealand. This
selection copyright © 1990 by Granta Publications Ltd.

Cover by the Senate. Photo: Tom Stoddart (Katz Pictures).

Granta 33, Summer 1990

ISBN 0-14-013859-5

CONTENTS

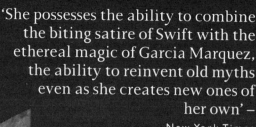

WILLIAM McPHERSON
IN ROMANIA

William McPherson

ate last December I flew to Berlin with a friend. It was an
impulse—I wanted to see the Wall while it was still
standing—and for the first time in some years, maybe in
my life, I was free to act on an impulse of that sort. My wish was
to spend the week between Christmas and the New Year in
Berlin, and in return· I promised my friend that we would spend
the next week in Italy, all of which we did: New Year's Eve at the
Brandenburg Gate, a week overlooking the Grand Canal in
Venice, then a few days in Florence and Rome. She returned to
New York, and I went back briefly to the luxury of Venice,
intending to go on to Budapest and Prague, return to Berlin once
more and so to home. Pan Am offered a special rate.

But plans have a way of changing. The images of the
Romanian revolution—I had seen it on television in Berlin—were
still vivid in my mind. I had a few extra days, after all. The
country was not far away. I got a copy of a map of Timişoara
and secured a visa to Romania. I rented a car and loaded it with
bananas, oranges and chocolate. A friend supplied me with some
telephone numbers in case of an emergency, a couple of cartons
of Kents—for purposes of bribery only; at the time I was not
smoking—and two bottles of Johnny Walker Red should the
Kents prove insufficient. And then, on 22 January, one month to
the day after Ceauşescu had fled by helicopter from the roof of
the Central Committee Building in Bucharest, I set off in my
newly rented Volkswagen Golf, equipped even with an extra can
of diesel fuel: just enough, I was told, to get me through
Romania without having to pay the prices the government was
charging foreigners for poor quality *motorină*.

I arrived at the Romanian border at four-thirty in the
afternoon, darkness already fast approaching. It was very cold.
Customs was taking a long time inspecting the Italian aid convoy
ahead of me. Finally after half an hour it was my turn.

'Any weapons? Drugs? Ammunition?' the customs official
asked.

'No, nothing.'

He inspected the car and asked me to open the hood. I
fumbled around under the dashboard in all the likely places but

couldn't figure out how to do it. I had neglected to look at the car very closely when I rented it, and now it was dark. I tried to find my flashlight but couldn't, and I felt like a fool.

'Is best you stop your travels tonight in Timişoara,' he said, more in the tone of an order than a suggestion. 'No more far.'

Yes, I assured him, pressing an orange into his hand, the Hotel Continental. 'I have a reservation.'

'Is the best.' He flashed me a V-sign; I returned it, and so I was off, but not for long. A couple of hundred metres up the road a soldier waved me to a stop.

'*Parlez-vous français?*' he asked. His French was about as fluent as mine.

'*Un peu.*'

'*Venez-vous aider la Roumanie?*'

He was rubbing his hands for warmth and looking at the oranges on the seat beside me. I showed my passport again, flashed the V-sign and gave him an orange. And after negotiating another impromptu border check-point, and another, dispensing more oranges and exchanging more V-signs, I was on my way to Timişoara, sixty-five kilometres distant. The road was better than I had expected and free of traffic, but very dark; even in the villages there was no light. All Romania was dark, I was soon to discover, and Timişoara, when I arrived there an hour later, seemed the darkest city I had ever seen.

I turned a corner, lost, and drove directly into the middle of a demonstration. The crowd filling the boulevard looked angry—perhaps a thousand people, maybe more, shouting, shoving, shaking their fists. I did not know if they were for the government or against the government. What was worse, I did not know if they were for or against me. I had no idea what they were shouting. I knew not a word of Romanian at that time, nor did I know that I had come to a stop in front of the former committee building of the district's Communist Party—the Council Building, as it was called. I knew only that I had been driving for half an hour or so in a city without lights and that I was lost. I hoped the people were friendly. They let me pass, in any event, and with relief I continued cruising the streets of Timişoara, searching for the Hotel Continental.

I recognized the triple-towered cathedral from newspaper photographs. On the steps of that cathedral, it had been reported, the terrorists fired on children holding a candle-light vigil, and the cathedral doors were locked against them. The report, I learned later, was a fabrication, but I did not know that then and I was startled by the sudden sight of it, and moved, surprising myself. I decided to give up my search for the hotel for the moment, park the car and go for a walk.

In the long square between the cathedral and the opera, clusters of candles were burning, and here and there dark figures in groups of two and three and four huddled together in the cold, whispering. No one looked at me directly. I passed the burning candles—hundreds of them—and the piles of evergreen boughs and the wreaths for the dead in the square. There were smashed windows and burnt shops and tanks with the soldiers peering out. I was caught somewhere between shock and awe and horror and tears, and I was a little nervous, too. Moreover, I was very cold. I decided to find the hotel.

Children and gypsies and money-changers thronged the parking lot. All of them wanted something: *gume*, *ciocolată*, dollars, especially dollars. One of the money-changers said something that made me laugh. I was grateful for that, but I wasn't going to deal with the first black-marketeer I saw and I continued to the entrance. There were soldiers everywhere: on the steps, at the doorway, in the lobby, around the reception desk. They looked so young, all with rifles casually slung over their shoulders. I showed my documents, registered and was given the key to room 108 where I was to spend the night. When I opened the door I was met by a blast of frigid air. Although it was very cold outside—a damp, penetrating cold—the windows were flung open wide. As it turned out, I spent many weeks in that hotel on four different occasions and with a single exception, when I checked in for only one night, I was assigned to 108, two doors down from the soldiers in 106 who were guarding the radio equipment that was housed, oddly enough, in a room twelve floors above. And the windows were always open when I arrived. Eventually, I grew rather fond of that room, of Mariana who cleaned it, even of the soldiers down the hall, but the first sight was not reassuring. It was too cold to stay there, so I left for another walk. And that is how I met Costel.

Costel was the black-marketeer—the 'businessman'—who had made me laugh. A slight man, in his twenties but almost completely bald, he was waiting on the steps in his sharp Italian jacket when I emerged, and still wanting to change money. The official rate at that time was ten *lei* to the dollar, which made Romania a very expensive place. I did not know what the unofficial rate was, but I was still not interested. I was going for a walk and invited Costel to come along.

Costel had learned his English from films and popular music, and it was primitive at best, but he managed to communicate in a smattering of French, Italian, English and a German word or two punctuated by his all-purpose expletive 'Jesus!', which was invariably accompanied by a sharp blow to the head with the heel of his hand. The expletives were very frequent. We walked to the Opera Square. This time I saw the bullet holes. The Opera itself was opening in two days for the first time since the Revolution with *Cavalleria Rusticana*. We moved on to Liberty Square where the army has its headquarters—more candles and crosses and wreaths marking the spot where the first victim fell in December—and on to the Square of the Union. All was deserted and dark. It was also cold, and I was hungry, so I invited Costel to my room for something to eat.

Costel tried to explain what had happened in Timişoara, 'the first free city in Romania,' from the Day of Sixteen to the Day of Twenty-two—as the days of the Revolution are everywhere called here—but the events were confusing and the language was a problem. We talked about money, an easier subject. The price of bread was five *lei* for a kilogram, and fuel cost nine *lei* a litre. The ration for the month of December was twenty-one litres;

13

sometimes it was eleven. Life was miserable and money was dear. Naturally he had to 'make business.' I suspect he was quite good at it. Three pages of my notebook are full of his calculations and figures.

I woke up early the next morning. The fog was very thick, and softened and reduced all colour. The outlines of the cathedral loomed at the far end of the square, the green light of its clock like the eye of Cyclops looking down. There were silent people moving past, candles glowing in the mist, and long, slow queues. Having nothing better to do, I joined the longest, which led down a stairway, underground. I could not see what lay at the head of the line—perhaps it was only a public toilet—but when I got down the steps there was a man selling newspapers. I was astonished to see such a long line for newspapers. I bought one of each, perhaps four or five in all. Encouraged by this success, I decided to join every line I saw. One just forming grew quickly to be longer than the first. When I realized that the people were lining up for one-kilogram tins of meat, the gift of an Italian aid mission—four to a person, a great luxury—I left and joined a line for apples. I wanted only one. I held out my hundred-*lei* note. How much? The man wanted to give it to me. I insisted. He refused. I took the apple and ate it as I walked back to the hotel for breakfast.

The coffee was terrible. I wrote in my notebook: next time tea. I look at that note now and suddenly I realize its implications. Had I already decided to spend another night in Timişoara? I had only the morning here. I mustn't waste it. I went into a shop. There were many clerks but only two customers and almost nothing to buy. Outside a man sat down on the pavement and pulled two flapping geese out of a valise. In a food shop, an *alimentară*, the shelves held tomato paste, raspberry syrup and mineral water, nothing else. I moved on, back to the Opera Square, past a poster for *A Comedy of Errors*, past the tanks now laden with flowers, towards the candles, the hastily erected crosses, the wreaths, into the cathedral. I bought a few more candles and lit them. For the Revolution. For the people

who had died in the square. For these sad faces I saw around me.
A boy followed me. He could not have been more than eight or
ten. He was a clever little boy with an engaging but somehow
twisted face. I supposed he had had some kind of injury. He
wanted money. I had only hundred-*lei* notes, and I gave him one.
He brought over his two pals. I parted with 200 more. Then they
asked for *gume-gume* and *ciocolată*. I had neither and I left the
cathedral, but not before surreptitiously dropping another
hundred *lei* on each of the cripples beside the door. By now I was
feeling both guilty for having so much money and foolish for
dropping it for every plaintive face. I had started out the morning
with 700 *lei* in my pocket. I had eighteen and a half left. I decided
to stay another night. I wanted to know what lay behind these
faces—as if another night would tell me.

Another young boy was standing beside me. He was well
dressed, wearing a fur hat. I took him to be about twelve. He was
eating a cookie, and he offered me one from the sack in his hand.
I took it. I was hungry again. I tried to speak with him, but he
spoke no English, no French. He did not utter a word in fact, but
he offered me another cookie, and together we moved on,
walking through the square. I was beginning to feel guilty for
eating so many of his cookies, and by signs I indicated lunch and
pointed towards the hotel. I took him into the dining-room and
we sat down to lunch, in silence. We had not exchanged a word,
but I wanted him to write his name in my notebook. I pointed to
myself and wrote 'Bill'. I pointed to him and handed him the pen.
He wrote in the Romanian fashion, last name first: 'Rotaru
Viorel. *Clasa* VII-A.'

Suddenly Costel, my money-changer from the night before,
rushed to the table. There was someone he wanted me to meet.
George. George spoke English. George had something to tell me.
Something important. He had people I must meet. He was
waiting in the lobby. Come! Come! Costel was pulling at my arm,
and I went to meet George. Costel vanished. The three of
us—George, Viorel and I—set off down the street. I couldn't
figure out exactly who George wanted me to meet, or why, but in
a few moments I was hustled into an old building where two or

three newspapers shared offices and everyone was speaking at
once. George was gone. Viorel had disappeared at the door. I
never saw him again, and I am sorry about that. Now that I
know enough words in Romanian, I would like to thank him for
the cookies, I would like to know how he is doing.

The newspaper offices were filled with cigarette smoke. The
people there were mostly young, many of them
students—writers and editors from a number of papers,
including the newspaper *Timişoara* whose first issue I had
bought, quite inadvertently, for half a *lei* in the square that
morning.

Tell us about democracy! they said.

We know nothing about democracy!

We need books, newspapers about democracy!

This is the first free town in Romania!

They say one in five people here is a *Securist*! Who can we
trust?

I was ushered from one room to another. The men and
women in those rooms—mostly men—seemed at once diffident
and very proud and more than a little anxious. Everything was
rushed—there was so little time, they told me, and so much to
learn, so much to do. They had started very late. They wanted to
talk about literature and art and life in the West and—a question
very often asked in Romania—how much had I paid for my
camera. They wanted to know which of my country's writers I
admired, and why. One young student with a shy but engaging
smile told me *Catcher in the Rye* was his favourite book. Some of
them had read Steinbeck—the old regime found him more
politically correct than most—and they were familiar with
Hemingway and Walt Whitman. I thought they knew a lot. And
I? What did I know of their country? Was I familiar with the
work of Brancuşi? Had I heard of Mircea Eliade? Mihai
Eminescu? They asked a lot of questions. They smoked a lot of
cigarettes. They laughed a lot, too. There was some joy in
Romania after all; or at least a sense of humour.

2

Petru, a reporter for the local student newspaper, *Forum Studențesc*, was impatient; he had something to show me. He rushed me down the stairs and out the door. We jumped on to a tram. 'No,' he said, when I pulled out some money for the fare, 'I am a revolutionary, I am a student. We do not pay.' So I did not pay either. Over the next few months I rode many trams in Timişoara; I rarely saw anyone pay.

Petru was a very nervous student of engineering, tall and thin with bloodshot eyes. He told me he had not slept for two days and I believed him. He pulled me aside. The document in his hand had been taken, he told me, from the desk of an important officer in the *Securitate*. It was three or four pages long and it contained a numbered list of names, informers—130 or 140 in all—the date each had been recruited and from where, and the amount of money each was paid.

'This is very dangerous. Tell no one. I am dead if they know I have this.'

Dead? Was he serious? I found it hard to believe, but I have since seen many things in Romania, even a suicide, that are hard to believe. 'Why are you showing this to me?'

'You are a journalist. I trust no one here. You must help.'

'But how?' I didn't know if I were slipping into reality or out of it. In Romania, I was beginning to learn, reality has a sliding floor. I looked at the document now in my hand. 'How do you know it's authentic?' I turned the pages. I turned the pages again. The names meant nothing to me. 'Petru, this is a copy. It is very easy to fake a copy.'

'Fake?'

'Falsify. Counterfeit.'

'No! It is veritable. I have a tape cassette, too. More dangerous. In a safe place. Oh! I am a dead man!'

'No, Petru. You're very much alive. I am your friend.' Not, I realized, that that would make much difference; I just wanted it to. 'You will be all right.' I looked again at the document. The list was in chronological order beginning four or five years before. It appeared to be written in the same spidery hand—until the end. There a line had been drawn part way across the page and three more names had been added beneath it, with a darker pen, by another hand. Someone had torn the original in half; the pages had been pieced back together to be copied.

Yes, Petru said, the officer of the *Securitate* was disposing of the document at the time of the Revolution. He had torn it.

'You took it out of his waste basket?'

No, he was in a great hurry. He tore it up and left it on his desk.

'For someone to find?' I asked. 'Look, Petru, this may be authentic, but it looks to me like a plant.'

'A plant?' He took the pages from my hand.

'Someone wanted you to find this.' But what kind of person, I asked myself, would plant such a thing, and what would he hope to achieve? The answer was not comforting.

'No. It is correct.' Petru folded the document and returned it carefully to his briefcase. I regret that I never saw it again. He produced a copy of his newspaper, laying it open before me. His name appeared at the top of the page above three poems. 'I am a poet. Please, I want you to have them.' He looked very proud.

That night there was a big demonstration. George, I noticed, had appeared at my side.

'What's happening, George?'

'The worms are leaving the apple.' George took my pen and notebook. 'I show you.'

He drew two worms abandoning an apple eaten to the core, and labelled it 'PCR'—Romanian Communist Party. The worms were headed for another apple, round and fat, labelled 'FSN'—*Frontul Salvării Naţionale*, the Front for National Salvation. George shrugged. 'The first apple is finished. They're going for the second.' It was as succinct an explanation of what was happening in Timişoara that week—and what had been happening in all of Romania since a few hours after Ceausescu fled—as any I heard.

At that moment in Timisoara there were two factions vying

for power and a third—the army—that seemed to be more or less holding it. The first president of the County Council after the Revolution had resigned—been forced out, really—on 12 January. That day was a day of mourning throughout Romania for the martyrs of the Revolution and one of massive demonstrations against the participation of former Communists in the government. That day the army under General Gheorghe Popescu had taken control of the city. General Popescu, an avuncular looking man with a paunch, had come out of retirement until local elections could be held.

Such a description makes the situation sound so clear. Maybe it was, but that evening and for many evenings to come it was far from clear to me. It wasn't clear to a lot of other people either, which was reassuring in a sense. Soldiers were stationed at the airport, the government buildings, the hospitals, the hotels, the opera—all the important points—but the army in control? The troops looked too young to control anything; the greatest danger appeared to be from one of their rifles going off by accident. The *Securitate* was still at large—there had been shooting, I was told—yet no one knew who or where they were. Who was who was difficult to sort out in Romania.

Two things were clear in Timişoara, however: everyone was a revolutionary, and no one wanted communism. No one wanted to lose what meagre privileges he had, either. And in Bucharest the Council of the National Salvation Front was consolidating its power. Originally, the Council was not a party—it had been only an interim arrangement of the Revolution—but that day it endorsed the decision, contrary to an earlier pledge, to field its own candidates in the national elections, now scheduled for 20 May. They didn't want to lose their privileges either.

Later in the evening, George invited me to his apartment. There had been a large and boisterous demonstration for the 'new' local Front, which was opposed to the previous night's *manifestation* for the 'old' Front, and George tried to explain the difference, again with the help of sketches. The old Front was composed of people who happened to congregate inside the Opera—the centre of the Revolution—from the Day of Seventeen onwards. All sorts of people, George said. Opportunists. Gypsies. Vagabonds. Rubbish people. Some good people, too. They formed the first post-revolutionary government of the county and of the city of Timişoara. But there were problems, and new councils would be elected soon. The elections were supported by Renaşterea, the 'independent' newspaper. It all sounded very democratic, except for the troubling worms in the apple.

The man behind the local elections in Timişoara was George's friend Savu. His given name was Ion, but I never heard anyone refer to him other than by his family name, Savu. Savu was the president of the Front in his enterprise, the detergent plant, one of the largest in Timişoara. Savu was a hero of the Revolution. He tried to make democracy in his factory. He had to run, hide. Even now. Five different houses in four days. 'Come! You must talk to him.' So George and Alec Russell, who had simply hopped a flight to Romania ten days before and was now filing for the *Daily Telegraph*, piled into my car and raced through the streets, black as pitch and dense with fog and riddled with pot-holes, to Savu's block, George shouting directions at the same time as he was shouting politics. I drove over a median strip. I couldn't see it in the fog. At times I wasn't even sure I was on a street. But we made it to Savu's, just as Savu was leaving for the railroad station.

Savu was catching the 11:54 to Bucharest. We sped to the train, jumping aboard with him, his wife and his retinue. There must have been six or eight of us jammed in the small space between the cars.

'Interview him,' George commanded.

I looked at my watch. The train wouldn't leave for more than an hour. 'Why are you going to Bucharest?' I asked.

'Timişoara is the first free town in Romania,' Savu said. I already knew that. 'From the beginning I fought for a real democracy. To fight with all my being for the rights of the people.' The fog was swirling. The locomotives were steaming. George was translating.

'Why are you going to Bucharest?'

'I do not want power. I have no interest in power.'

'But why are you going to Bucharest?'

'One. For an exact determination of political intentions for the short and long term. Two. For help for a real democracy. Timişoara is the . . . ' My notes are scarcely decipherable, but really it made no difference. I had heard many politicians, and although Savu's life might well have been in danger, he sounded like a politician to me. 'One. Really free elections without any pressure from different groups, without interference of private interests. Only honest people. I do not want power.'

'How do you determine who is honest?'

'I was elected by the workers. I am president of the Front in my enterprise. Timişoara will be the first town with democracy in Romania.'

I am not quite sure why I asked the next question. Perhaps I had surmised the situation. Savu had, after all, been living like a fugitive. 'Do you trust anyone?'

'No.'

'No one at all?'

'Only Marton Florin.' (I met Florin a couple of days later. He was a football player, an engineer, and of course a revolutionary. I liked him. A few days after that, he said it was urgent to speak to me. When he came to my room he was so terrified he could not talk, not in my room—it might be bugged—and not outside, either. Maybe I could meet him in Belgrade. I didn't see Florin again for four months, not until after the national elections in May, when he seemed relaxed and quite content. He had been invited to Bucharest where he met Mr Iliescu; he had been made president of the Sports Club of his factory—that was his job. He had voted for Mr Iliescu and life was good and the National Salvation Front was 'the best.')

Savu amended his statement: 'Maybe Marton Florin.' I was learning my first lesson about Romania: no one trusts anyone.

3

As it happened, I did leave Romania—for the afternoon. I drove to Belgrade with Alec, the young journalist from Britain, and Corina, a translator who had never been out of her country. She had never seen shops full of oranges and bananas and chocolate and coffee. She had never seen a city illuminated at night. We went, in short, so that Corina could buy fruit, which she did, masses of it; so that she could use her fresh new passport, her first; so that she could see a city with lights. Belgrade is not Paris by day or by night, and its shops are not luxurious by the standards of London or New York, but it sufficed. After my short time in Timişoara—amazing how quickly the eye grows accustomed to its surroundings—Belgrade looked splendid enough to Alec and me as well. So we all bought fruit, and had coffee and cakes in a café, and then later had dinner in a fairly ordinary cafeteria where, I thought, I lost my red scarf. It was a favourite scarf. I had bought it in London a few years before. We looked around the restaurant, we searched the car. The next day I searched the car again. Someone in Belgrade, I thought, has a very nice scarf. I never expected to see it again, but I did, a few weeks later, when Corina came to visit me in my hotel room where I was recuperating from a particularly virulent case of food poisoning. The scarf was around her neck. I let it pass.

The local elections in Timişoara were held the last Saturday and Monday of January. The new Front replaced the old on the councils of the municipality and the county. No one was surprised, although many were unhappy, and on the Sunday between the two elections there was a very big demonstration. '*Jos Iliescu! Jos comunismul!*' the people chanted; 'Down with Iliescu! Down with communism! We are not rats. We do not want a new perestroika. *Libertate! Libertate!*'

George, I noticed, had appeared at my side.

'What's happening, George?'

'Nobody knows exactly.'

It seemed to me, though, that a lot of people in Timişoara

were objecting to the early retirement of the December revolutionaries—many of them young people—in favour of the considerably older order of Party bureaucrats and chiefs and masters who had run the farms, factories, enterprises and lives of people before, and were about to run them again.

Both days the balloting took place in the Olimpia Sports Hall, under the supervision of the Committee for Free Elections, which the old Front did not recognize. The entrance was guarded by soldiers. Savu was there, plump and proud, making politics in a red tie and pin-stripe jacket. His wife and various other members of the Committee were seated behind a large table on the floor. The elections were not like elections I was accustomed to in the West. The citizens of Timişoara did not turn out to vote. A fellow I had met three days before asked me where I was going that Saturday morning. To the elections, I said.

'What elections?' he asked.

The electoral procedures had been set up in four days the week before; the dates had been established on Wednesday, the day Savu was in Bucharest. The old Communist cells in every factory had disappeared, of course, on 22 December. They were replaced, more or less, by the new and revolutionary-sounding fronts, who chose the delegates—about 1,000 in all—who then chose the candidates and elected the members of the Municipal Council and the larger and more powerful County Council.

But exactly how this system worked was difficult to figure out. 'So every four hundred workers in an enterprise get one delegate for the county elections and two for the city?'

George nodded, but his assent seemed weak.

'And every ten to twenty delegates name one candidate?'

George nodded again. 'Maybe. Is not for sure.'

Few things were 'for sure'. But the voting was very orderly, the ballot boxes were sealed, unsealed, the ballots counted and the results announced. Savu told us we had just witnessed the first free elections in Timişoara, indeed, in all Romania, since 1928, and the first ever done with the help of computers. In making this announcement Savu looked pleased as Punch.

George smiled. He is a good-looking man, and he has an

engaging smile. 'What you see is not true,' he said, 'and what is true you cannot see, only feel. That is what Romania was before, and it still is.' He laughed; George enjoys being cryptic. 'Reality is a secret here.'

'Now we have the celebration,' declared the President of the Committee for Free Elections, his voice jubilant, and late that rainy Monday afternoon we all marched over to the cathedral. Amid the chanting of the choir and the swirl of incense and the flaming candles and the priests in white and gold, my new friend Emil whispered in my ear, 'The bishop who blessed Ceauşescu now blesses the new Council.'

From the cathedral we went to the Council Building where, amid some commotion and many soldiers bearing rifles, the newly elected County Council replaced the old. During this transfer of power—remarkably orderly, under the circumstances—a young man burst into the chamber. 'Something very important is happening on television! They're massing in Bucharest for the Front!'

We rushed out to the television. The Prime Minister, Petre Roman, was speaking from the floodlit balcony. The workers were chanting:

> *Noi sîntem uniţi*
> *Nu sîntem platiţi!*

> We are united,
> We are not paid!

But everyone else had rushed to the television too, and it was hard to see, and I did not at that moment understand the reference.

Later that night and during the next, I began to understand what I had glimpsed on television. It was not just another manifestation. There had been massive anti-Front demonstrations in Bucharest the previous day, and for the first time the government had responded by calling out the workers for a show of support. Among those workers, though not then in great numbers, were miners from the Valley of the Jiu.

There had been rumours—rumours that the Front carefully planted, it was said—of an orchestrated *putsch*, and that the two principal opposition parties, the Peasant and Liberal parties, had paid the protesters 200 *lei* each. That is why the workers were chanting, 'We are united, we are not paid!' But there were also stories that they were paid a week's wages and given the day off.

Three nights later, three miners appeared on Free Romanian Television, urging everyone to go back to work and let the Front run the government. The Front is the leader, they said, not one or another of the opposition parties. Iliescu himself said he saw no need for more than one party. None the less, the government eventually agreed to form a sort of coalition with other parties in a Provisional Council of National Unity that would rule until the national elections in May. There was little question as to which party—the Front had now declared itself a party—would control the Council.

The miners and various other workers got a raise. The protests briefly subsided, though they did not disappear, and I left Timişoara for a time.

4

I went to Bucharest for a week and then to the historic Transylvanian town of Alba Iulia to visit the parents of Emil, the man who had spoken to me in the cathedral on the night of the local elections. Emil—like many others in Romania—proudly described himself as the son of peasants. His parents had come from a nearby village but had given up their land during the forced collectivization and moved to the city. Emil's father was a shoe-maker and his mother a dressmaker. Emil was their only child. For many years his father had walked to work instead of taking the bus to save two *lei* a day so they could provide some advantages—books, clothes—for their son. They were not poor—they never had been poor peasants, which had caused them some problems—and they owned their three-room apartment. They certainly were not rich, either, though they were fortunate by the standards of most Romanian peasant families. They were intelligent and very generous, and they were concerned about the violence and the confusion in Bucharest. There was a great fear of anarchy and disorder in Romania, a fear the government skilfully played on.

The day I arrived there—Monday, 19 February—the miners had come to Bucharest again. This time there were thousands of them. I was sitting in Emil's parents' living-room watching television. His parents were concerned—not so much about the miners, whose violence was not shown on television, but about the students: 200 putative students had invaded government headquarters on the Sunday before and briefly seized the Deputy Prime Minister. Some armed with clubs devastated offices in the building. Those short, chaotic scenes were shown many times. It was impossible to tell from the television how many students were involved or even if they were students. The word '*putsch*' occurred again. Iliescu said the students were counter-revolutionary, against the national interests. 'We don't know who they were but we will search for them and punish them severely,' he said. In the meantime, 'We appeal to all interested forces, to all clear minds, to protect us, because we are leading the country.'

Emil's father shook his head. What to think?

'A manipulation!' Emil cried. 'Another manipulation!' Apparently the invading students met only perfunctory resistance from the army and the police. Curious. Was this Iliescu's wish, in order to convince the populace that the Revolution was in danger and thus justify the measures he needed to take to stay in power? Were the army and the police plotting something?

'The wolves have changed their fur but not their habits,' Emil said. 'The frames are the same.' Emil's father shook his head again. His mother urged more food on me. We drank a little *ţuica*.

5

One Saturday afternoon in the middle of March I drove to Petroşani, a mining town in the Valley of the Jiu, with Emil and Ionel, another friend. I wanted to see what these miners were like. I wanted to go into a mine. We were having car trouble and while Emil and Ionel peered under the hood—all Romanians are by necessity auto mechanics—I walked up the street. The mining towns were meant to be grim places. Petroşani didn't look that bad to me, but I had been in Romania long enough by then to have grown accustomed to bleakness. There were few people on the streets, but the sun was shining, which always helps.

While I was walking up the street, a taxi-driver had come over to peer under the hood, and Emil had told him I wanted to visit a coal-mine. By the time I returned to the car a man came running up, excited, breathless. He looked about thirty, not tall but husky. A businessman, I thought. He wants to change money. But no. He wanted to practise his English, which he had learned from the movies.

'Los Angeles,' he said. 'California.'

His English was fairly rudimentary. He was a miner and his name was Ion, and he would take me into a mine. He had a mask for me, and a lamp, and clothes. He would show me a real mine; I would see what it was like.

'No problem,' Ion said. 'Just not speak.'

'Not speak?'

'You are miner, not tourist. Most not journalist.'

'Oh.' I pondered that. 'What do you mean? I can't talk?'

'Simple. Be miner. I show you.'

'And if someone speaks to me?'

'Simple. Just not speak.'

'Oh.' I looked at Emil. Emil shrugged. Not his problem. I was the one who wanted to go into a mine.

I'd be going alone, too, or at least without Emil. Ion had only one spare outfit. It became clear that I would have to stay there the whole shift, which began at ten that night. I would go to the head of the mine with Ion, leave my clothes, and put on the suit he had for me. 'Remember, you are Romanian miner.'

'But my clothes, Ion. These aren't Romanian clothes.'

'How much you pay for the jacket?' Ion asked.

'That's what I mean,' I said. Ion looked puzzled.

'How much?'

I was certain now that this adventure was ill-advised. But no. Ion would arrange it. 'No problem,' if only I remembered not to speak. Just pick up my tools and act like a miner. He invited us to his apartment to discuss it, and to tell me his story.

Ion was the son of a simple miner from Moldavia. Like his father, Ion was not a specialist. He showed me his salary slip. He was paid 4,900 *lei* a month, including extra money for night work. Specialist miners are paid double that, and more. This is far above the wage of most Romanians, who make around 3,000 *lei* a month. Miners paid less for electricity too. None the less, I never met anyone who wanted to change places with a miner. Ion's rent for the one-room apartment he shared with his wife and daughter was 200 *lei* a month. The apartment contained, in addition to a glassed cabinet along one wall, a sofa that made into a bed, a table with three wooden chairs around it and a large television set. Ion was proud of the television set. He wanted to be photographed in front of it, with his wife, with the set turned on. He didn't own a car, but he wished for a motor cycle.

One day last August he'd been on a motor cycle. An American from California was passing through. Admiring the motorcycle and eager to practise his English, Ion spoke to him. The American took Ion's photograph on the bike—he showed me the picture—and later that day a member of the *Securitate* came to his door: the photograph had been taken in front of the *Securist's* house.

The man asked Ion how he knew English and what he had told the foreigner. Then he proposed that Ion work for them as an informer for 800 *lei* a month, in addition to his wages from the mine. Ion refused. The man took his identity card. The next day was pay-day at the mine; to collect his wages, Ion needed his identity card. The *Securitate* man showed up with it. Again he asked him to co-operate, and again Ion refused. Two weeks later

Coal-washing plant at Vulcan.

two men from the *Securitate* came to his house and accused him of stealing bikes. They then left. They returned and told him they knew he was dealing in the black-market. He had better co-operate.

'Come to my house and see,' Ion had said. 'They see empty bottles of whisky.' He gestured toward the cabinet. 'I picked them out of the rubbish.' The bottles were displayed behind glass, along with spray cans of deodorant and perfume, boxes of Marlboros and Gitanes. All of them were empty. The *Securişti* didn't come again.

I asked Ion if he'd gone to Bucharest with the miners in February.

Yes, he had. A boss had asked him to go and he had taken one of the trains from Petroşani that night. At every station, he said, they were greeted by townspeople bringing them hot bread, yoghurt, coffee and Romanian cigarettes.

'The same food at every stop?'

'Yes.' The same cigarettes too. No, the government didn't organize the people; the people wanted to help.

'They say we were paid by the Front to go to Bucharest.' I hadn't asked. 'No, never. We were never paid. The heart went to Bucharest.'

'Why?'

'I see the television. I see what happened in the government building. It makes me nervous. Upset. How can I go to work, feeling like that? If I make a mistake, 5,000 or 10,000 people are dead. Let's say so.'

It occurred to me to wonder what would happen if I went down the mine that night and made a mistake, but I didn't pursue it. 'What happened in Bucharest?'

'In Bucharest everyone was crying out, "Up with Iliescu! Up with the Front!" My heart went to Bucharest.'

'Do you like Iliescu, Ion?'

'A hard question.' Ion shrugged, thought for a moment. 'Yes, I like Iliescu. He gives us a thirty-day holiday minimum. He tells us we can retire at forty-five. Before, it was fifty-five. He gives us equipment for working. We do not have to pay for it.'

But they had been on strike. 'Why?'

'They had promised us things, and they had not come through. They had promised our wages would go up thirty-five per cent. We got fifteen. After the strike Iliescu had promised us everything, only go to work again. But nothing changed. No changes, only promises. So the miners strike.'

'Only promises,' Emil said. 'They change their name but not their habits.'

'The old Communist mafia is still in power,' Ion said agreeing. 'The mayor, he's one. The directors of the mines, they just switched them to other mines.'

'They changed their mines but not their habits,' Emil said.

'The man who was director of my mine, now he's mayor of the county. It's a better job.'

Ion got up to get me his spare miner's lamp and a mask. I worked the lamp and tried on the mask. It smelled of coal. I tried to imagine myself in the role of a mute Romanian miner. I couldn't quite. 'I do not have an extra safety hat,' Ion said. 'My colleague will give me one.'

'I think I won't go into the mine tonight, Ion. It will be too late, and I must be in Bucharest tomorrow. Perhaps another time.'

'You will come back?'

'I'll try.'

'When you come back, I like Gitanes, postcards, newspapers. But don't ask at the police where I am located. The old mafia still works. Ask at the taxi.'

I took the photograph of Ion and his wife in front of the television, and another in front of the whisky bottles in the cabinet. We exchanged addresses, shook hands and parted. I didn't think to ask Ion if he would return to Bucharest should the need arise. But I suppose the answer was clear. Anyway, I intend to go back to Petroşani. I'll ask him then.

Traditional miners' funeral procession.

Photo: James Nubile (Impact)

Petrila Mine.

Shift-change at Petrila Mine in the Jiu Valley.

6

The last demonstration in Bucharest was eight weeks long and began on a pleasant Sunday night in April, the same night that a nearly complete version of the trial of Nicolae and Elena Ceauşescu was shown on Free Romanian Television for the first time, keeping most citizens occupied until after ten. That night the demonstration looked no different from any other I had seen in Romania. It was more peaceful than most. At eleven o'clock, when I arrived in University Square, the speeches had ended and the riot police had already left. The demonstrators barricaded the square and had remained there throughout the night. In the early hours, the police returned with dogs and truncheons, and arrested sixty or seventy people. At that hour there were few witnesses.

The next evening 5,000 people were milling in the square. Shortly after midnight a man with a bull-horn said that a colonel of the *Poliţia* had appeared on television and accused the demonstrators of rape, theft, breaking into apartments on the square and damaging buses. The people there—I saw a number I knew—did not look like rapists and thieves to me. They looked like professional people, like students, like the residents of Bucharest one saw on the streets every day. They didn't even walk on the grass or the flowers. They just wanted the old Communists out of the government. That would have meant, of course, the end of the government, because as far as I could tell, everyone from Iliescu on down had been a Communist, most in important positions, although some like Iliescu had fallen into disfavour in recent years.

By the next evening there were 10,000 people. They were being led in a chant: 'Don't be frightened.'

'We won't.'

'Don't leave.'

'We won't.'

'Today the capital!'

'Tomorrow the whole country!'

Ten thousand shouting people make a very loud roar.

That night I was told, when I went into the University

building and up to the balcony of the Faculty of Geography and Geology where the leaders of the protest gathered, that the demonstration had started with a meeting to remember the dead. It had begun at the Cemetery of the Heroes and continued to the University Square, the Roman Square, the television station, where they asked that the decree subordinating the television to the government be rescinded. It was not. It never has been. The marchers returned to the square, where some of them at least remained, night and day, from that Sunday until the morning of 13 June, nearly two months later. Some set up tents near the National Theatre, and a number began a hunger strike. 'In this Square,' one of the leaders said, 'more than three hundred died on the Day of Twenty-one, and maybe two thousand were wounded. We will never leave until the Revolution is finished.'

They didn't, but a couple of days later I did. I wanted to be in Timişoara for the national elections on 20 May. I knew that Bucharest would be packed with journalists and foreign observers. It was already difficult to book a hotel room.

To the surprise of no one, the elections produced a landslide victory for Iliescu and the Front.

I returned to the capital early in the evening of 12 June, with Emil again, and checked into the Hotel Ambassador, some 500 metres up the street from University Square. In my room there, neither the telephone nor the television worked; its only advantage, aside from its justifiably lower price, was the balcony overlooking the Boulevard General Magheru, which becomes the Boulevard Nicolae Bălcescu in the next block. When I arrived, marchers were passing beneath the balcony, chanting: 'Sound asleep you voted in a dictator!' They were headed toward Victory Square and the headquarters of the government. I let them go by. I was tired. I had seen many marches. I was sure that in time they would come marching back, and four hours later they did. Besides, the crowd seemed to have changed. After the May elections the student leaders, in a gesture of conciliation (and because the students had exams to take), had called for official demonstrations only on Thursdays. The hunger-strikers remained, a few students and others, and traffic continued to be diverted around University Square, as it had been since the demonstration began. But the crowds were thin, and at night they seemed to consist less of *opozanţii* than of opportunists. The students—Iliescu's *golani*—had more or less withdrawn from the Square, leaving it to what the Prime Minister, Petre Roman, later described, and accurately enough, as the underworld of Bucharest—the *traficanţi*, the chiefs of prostitution and assorted other lowlife, the *dégradés* and *déclassés* as he called them, with which the city abounds. When I made a midnight visit to the square during a brief stay in Bucharest the week before, I had been offered—for dollars—whisky, cigarettes, two women and *lei*. The crowd was not the same.

The evening of 13 June began with an explosion. Someone had thrown a Molotov Cocktail—then another and another—and Emil and I rushed out to see. But it was raining and I ran back to the hotel room for my umbrella, absurdly enough, which is how I lost Emil.

I left the hotel moments later, running towards University Square, but Emil had disappeared. Buses were in flames, some still exploding. The stench of burning rubber filled the air. I ran faster, to the university building and up the stairs to the balcony.

'Don't go out!' someone shouted.

'But I must see,' and I went out. Burning buses were blocking the square, seven of them. The square itself was almost empty.

Someone from the Student League pulled me inside. 'No one must be seen on the balcony! It is dangerous. The Student League did not organize the violence! We must not be blamed!'

'But I just saw someone on the balcony. What happened?'

This is what happened. In the early hours of the morning, about 1,000 policemen in riot gear and armed with truncheons charged the barricades blocking University Square, forming a cordon and stopping the exits. Military police in combat fatigues then rushed in and, together with an undetermined number of plain-clothes men whom many found reminiscent of the old

Securitate, arrested eight or ten hunger-strikers and various others camped there, between 200 and 300 in all. Some time after five o'clock in the morning, the customary hour for the police to strike, the President of the Student League of the University of Bucharest, Marian Munteanu, was arrested in his home, as well as various others in their homes and at the Institute of Architecture. University Square was cleared of demonstrators, and soon workers were painting fresh traffic lines on the boulevard. By ten-thirty, women in babushkas were turning over the hard-packed earth in front of the National Theatre, in the place where the demonstrators had pitched their tents.

A woman appeared in the square a short time later and was dragged kicking into an unmarked car. An hour later workers from the IMGB, a large heavy-equipment enterprise in Bucharest, appeared and attacked the Institute of Architecture. There were a hundred or so students—some say gypsies, not students; they were probably both—hiding inside. The workers began pounding on the doors, crying that the IMGB was making order. A window was broken. An enormous crowd was forming around the back of the workers, shouting that Iliescu had sent his scandal makers. There was fighting. The police stood by. The workers surged once again towards the Institute, throwing rocks now, windows breaking. The police remained calm.

By late afternoon, demonstrators had become more violent and invaded the square again—thousands of them this time—more stones were thrown, and not long after that the Molotov cocktails. The remaining police ran away, and a few minutes after five o'clock I arrived, just as the student leader Marian Munteanu, who had been released shortly before, was concluding a plea from the balcony. March on the police headquarters to free the prisoners, Munteanu said, but '*Fără violenţe!*' Without violence! And so thousands of people set out for the Municipal Police Headquarters.

When I reached the headquarters, I saw that others had got there before me: the gatehouse was in flames, six vehicles were burning in the stone courtyard and the building itself was on fire. Many windows were broken. The building was dark and apparently deserted. Hundreds, maybe thousands, thronged the street that led to the headquarters' entrance, but the street directly in front of it was relatively clear: a man had been shot in the head there an hour before. Had I known that then, I might have been more cautious. But I didn't know it, and I went into the courtyard for a quick look. Six or eight young men were lounging on the steps, passing bottles of beer among them. They did not look like students.

The Internal Security Ministry was next to the police headquarters; across the street was the *Securitate*, a small, old and rather pretty brick building: they were burning too. Black smoke was pouring from the entrance of the nearby underground garage: more vehicles were on fire down there. A boy ran out, his eyes streaming tears. His four friends were still in the garage. It was impossible to get them out because of the smoke. 'I am the only one who escaped!' he shouted. There was another explosion—from the garage. Where were the police? Where was the army? They had run away, I was told. Strange.

8

It should have been a pleasant evening for a stroll. The air was fresh after the afternoon's rains. Passers-by, many with their children, were chatting, laughing. I walked along the Boulevard of Aviators towards Victory Square. The events of the afternoon, the events that I had myself witnessed, began to seem unreal. Had I really seen buses burning and buildings in flames and a boy whose eyes were streaming tears? 'It's all a movie,' Emil often said, referring to the events of the last six months. It gave a kind of false comfort to think so.

The scene at the massive Foreign Ministry, since the Revolution the seat of the government, was impressive: the darkened building squatting there, the broad floodlit square, the crowds milling. The people had come there, I soon learned, in response to Iliescu's plea that 'all conscious forces gather around the buildings of the government and the television to curb the attempts of the extremist groups to use force, and to defend the democracy that was so difficult to attain.' He had spoken ominously of an organized *coup d'état* in the offing. And so, at ten o'clock, as the long Bucharest twilight was finally giving way to night, there they were, the 'conscious forces', several thousand strong, helping each other don white arm bands.

I found a woman who spoke English. The white band, I said, pointing to her arm. What is it for?

'You don't know?' She seemed surprised. 'We support the Front. We are *Fesenişti*. This is our sign.' Then she told me about Mr Iliescu's call to the people, and that a mob had briefly seized the television station, cutting off transmission for more than an hour. 'Now we wait for Mr Iliescu.' I had passed within two blocks of the television station a few minutes before.

'You know what they did at the University Square?'

Yes, I knew.

'It will be a white night,' she predicted, a night without rest.

At two in the morning I was with two young British journalists—the few journalists now in Bucharest seemed all to be British, and most of them were young—and a translator. I had met them at the Hotel Intercontinental. We had all heard gunshots forty-five minutes before and went near the television station to investigate. We met four paratroopers.

No, there was no shooting here,' they said. 'Only rocks were thrown. The police had rubber truncheons only. Go home. We don't need you to write about Romania now.'

We tried another approach to the television station, failed, passed by the Foreign Ministry—'There was no shooting here; only at the television'—and then returned to the entrance to the Intercontinental. Church bells began to ring, then suddenly stopped. Almost immediately there was a round of gunfire. It seemed to be coming from the direction of the Interior Ministry. I ran to the corner of the Square, with Sorin whom I had just met and who was to become my friend. There was an ambulance from *Médecins sans Frontières*. A man had been shot in the chest—he looked near death—and another had been shot in the cheek. Everything was happening so quickly nothing had time to register. We ran across the square to the Boulevard Gheorghiu-Dej, where there was a burnt shell of a bus. Farther down the boulevard we could see tanks and a line of riot police with white shields and helmets and truncheons. We watched. Were the tanks moving? It was hard to tell. The street was dark, and we were looking at the tanks head on. Shots rang out. I saw the flames from the rifles.

'Run! Get down!' Sorin was screaming, pulling at my arm. We ran behind the ruined bus. 'They're using real bullets!' Sorin could hear the ricochet. I could not tell. I had never been in the military. I had never seen a war. The shooting stopped. Another French ambulance drove up, waiting. We moved cautiously out. More gunfire, and we ran again. Were the tanks moving?

'We go,' Sorin said, pulling at my arm again. And we ran around the corner, out of sight of the rifles, the tanks, the sheltering bus, and back to the front of the hotel.

We exchanged stories with the four or five journalists clustered there, watched the troops file across the street by the Geography Faculty. Suddenly the police made a running baton charge—they came within inches of us, out of nowhere. No one had seen them coming. No one saw what they were going after. It was three in the morning. We went to Alec Russell's room, which had a balcony with a good view of the square. Alec asked if I'd like to sleep on his couch.

Yes, I would. I was afraid to walk up the street to the Hotel Ambassador.

As I was drifting off, I thought I heard a strange soft noise, a kind of murmuring. I listened for a few moments, straining to hear—was that a sound, or was I imagining it?—then reluctantly pulled myself from the couch and went to the balcony once more. I looked down. I didn't see anything at first, only shadows. Then I didn't know what I was seeing. I didn't really want to see anything more. But why else was I here?—and I knew that what I saw down there was important.

'Alec, wake up! Come quick! Wake up! Alec!'

At five in the morning, in the hushed first light before the dawn, the first group of miners—only a few hundred then—were swarming down the broad Boulevard Nicolae Bălcescu from Victory Square towards the university. Shrouded in that early half-light, their dun-coloured shapes were muffled, indistinct, grey shadow on grey shadow and discernible at first only by the soft flickering of the lamps in their hands, on their metal helmets, and by the nervous rustling sound and a low buzzing hum that carried from the street to our balcony sixteen floors above.

A quarter of an hour later there were some thousands. Approaching the square the miners marched in phalanxes—several hundred in each—and when they arrived the phalanxes broke up, the flashing beams from thousands of tiny lamps darting restlessly in the shadow.

As the light increased, it became apparent that the miners were dressed for work, carrying the picks and chisels, augers and rubber hoses of their trade, as well as identical long sticks—and clubs, limbs torn from trees, pipes, iron bars, axes, chains—whatever came to hand that might be used to protect their government and restore order to the capital. And the humming voices we were hearing were calling for the objects of their hunt: *Golani! Golani!*

As they reached the Square a black Dacia with yellow licence plates came to a stop near the Hotel Intercontinental. Yellow plates indicate a government vehicle. Two men in suits were walking at the edge of the street, in the same direction as the miners. Secret police everywhere look the same.

A group of the miners broke off and rushed down to the entrance of the university building. Soon several miners appeared on the balcony of the Faculty of Geography and Geology, which occupies the eastern end of the university building, overlooking the square. The student protests, which began almost eight weeks before, were led from that balcony. It is a familiar landmark in Bucharest. A few soldiers—twenty or thirty—were standing casually on the sidewalk beneath it. There were no other army, or police, or riot squads. The miners reached the roof. Six or eight of them had climbed through one of the skylights and were waving triumphantly. The building appeared to be empty.

A few moments later a man wearing a red sweater appeared on the street, began to run and disappeared around a corner and out of sight, pursued by miners wielding sticks. A truck drove slowly into the square. Through a megaphone a voice boomed: 'Don't be afraid, the miners are good people.'

Several people were with us now, Romanian friends and journalists, including Hermann Tertsch from the Madrid newspaper *El Pais*. He had driven through the night from Bulgaria and seen the miners gathering at four-thirty in Victory Square before they began their march down the boulevard to the university. He also brought word from the reception desk: the miners said if they saw anyone taking photographs from the balconies they would come in and devastate the hotel. As we were hearing this, they captured a man near the fountain between the Geography Faculty and Institute of Architecture and beat him to the ground. A few minutes later, a fire was blazing up the street in front of the Liberal Party's headquarters. The flames reached the second storey, and we heard glass shattering, an occasional scream. On the street there was another announcement: 'Those of you who see cameras, catch the people and take them to the cars.' Apparently the 'cars' were the unmarked black and white Dacias we saw here and there around the hotel and the square. But there was no one on the street with a camera. No one would be foolish enough to appear on the street with a camera. No one not already in the street would be foolish enough to enter it.

We heard a rumour that there were 30,000 miners in Bucharest. It was hard to tell how many were in the square, at least 5,000. They were everywhere and more were arriving. By six o'clock the miners had invaded the Institute of Architecture—we could see them through the windows—and five of them now claimed the roof. A voice came over the hotel's public-address system: 'No more cameras.' At the same time, two men in blue suits, white shirts and ties, carrying briefcases, were talking affably to a group of miners, clapping them on their shoulders.

I took the elevator to the lobby. About 150 miners were standing at the door with clubs, logs and rubber hoses. They wanted mineral water and the hotel provided it. I did not go out but instead returned to the balcony in time to see the first marked police car arrive in the square.

By this time the miners had seized a number of people: they either beat them with sticks or dragged them into an unmarked vehicle or both; usually they did both. Someone suggested that their victims were being taken to the government building. I don't know how these rumours were reaching us. None of us had yet ventured outside the hotel. I suppose they were coming by telephone, through our Romanian friends. Cristian Unteanu, the government's press spokesman, was standing beside a car in the centre of the square.

Another announcement from the megaphone: 'All civilians out of the square! This is not a show here. You are not capable of making order in Bucharest. We'll do it our way now.'

At the edge of the square the miners were beating a man in the face with sticks, then they kicked him. They kicked him twice in the face, and then in the stomach, and then they clubbed him in the stomach. He was doubled over, bleeding, trying to protect himself. He was led to one of the waiting cars in the middle of the square. It took a long time because they were beating him. I wondered if this was what it had been like in Nazi Germany when the Brown Shirts were loose. A woman appeared to be on her way to work, but she was knocked to the ground, beaten, forced into a waiting car. Another man was being kicked in the face. The violence intensified, spread like an infection. Miners were shaking their fists at people on the balconies of the hotel, shouting 'Photos are forbidden!' Many were looking at us.

I returned to the lobby. It was seven-twenty. The miners had chased a man into the hotel's revolving door and were beating him with clubs, chains, hoses. He was slumped there, his face bleeding, which he was trying to protect with his hands. He was picked up and dragged to a waiting car. I stood in the doorway for a minute, venturing out a step or two. I wanted to make a list of the weapons I saw. Here is my list: thick chains, miner's drills (one came up to my chest; it was very thick and must have been five feet long), pipes, wooden clubs, tree limbs, rubber hoses with nozzles attached, chains in rubber hoses . . . I left before finishing the list, but in a few moments I went out again and stood under the canopy. I saw a miner carrying one of the distinctive yellow plastic 'Raţiu for President' bags. Ion Raţiu was the National Peasant Party's candidate. I assumed—correctly, as it happens—that they had invaded the party's headquarters nearby.

A little later several of us very cautiously ventured out, farther this time. We were in a group; we were safe, we thought. Stop. A little farther. Stop. More. We reached the steps leading to the sidewalk and the street. A woman in a red pullover and a dark skirt was running towards us, screaming, several miners surrounding her, chasing her, hitting her with clubs, tearing at her clothes. She lost one shoe, the other. Her pullover was ripped, then ripped off. She was naked to the waist, and they were beating her with whatever implements they had. I screamed at them—'Stop!'—but Sorin, the fellow I'd met the night before, clapped his hand over my mouth. All this happened very fast. The woman was running by me, or trying to. She was stumbling and they were beating her. She was no more than a body's length away, between our small cluster and the hotel. As she passed I saw a very large red bruise on her breast, and then I saw her back, which had been beaten raw, to a pulp. I had never seen anyone beaten to a pulp before. It had always seemed a cliché. Her skirt was torn, her legs were bleeding; her face was a blotch. She was pummelled, dragged and then pushed into a waiting vehicle. I was standing with Victoria Clark, a young woman who writes for the *Observer*. Victoria speaks some Romanian, and she had more nerve than I. We walked over to three or four miners and asked why they had beaten this woman.

She was on drugs, they told us. 'There is a lot of heroin here. We found this big bag on her.' With his hands he indicated something the size of a ten-pound sack of flour. None of us had ever seen a drug in Romania. None of us knew any Romanians who had.

'You tore off her clothes.'

'No, we found her like that.' They were carrying long steel augers. 'We are guardians of order, of peace, and we'll stay until we have peace.' And then the old revolutionary cry—Savu said

University Square, Bucharest, June 15 1990.

something like it on the Day of Twenty—'We die, we fight to defend you.'

Who were they defending us from?

'Prostitutes, drug addicts, fascists.'

How did they identify them?

'Pistols, drugs, bullets and inflammatory pamphlets—we found on all these people we have arrested.' But the miners didn't show us any.

Beside the entrance to the hotel fifty or sixty pieces of luggage were lined up. Inside, a large group of Japanese tourists, their faces quite impassive, were waiting to leave. The airport, I heard later, was closed. The miners wanted to check the hotel, room by room, for Marian Munteanu, the president of the Student League. He had been arrested the morning before but released to be arrested again. A reporter told us the miners had already found Munteanu. He saw them beating him in the square earlier.

Three or four of us decide to make a foray down the square. We began talking to a miner who showed us what he had confiscated from one of those arrested. (That was the word being used: arrested. It seemed a rather benign way to describe what was happening to people who had been clubbed and bloodied and thrown into unmarked cars and driven off.) He handed me a pamphlet containing the Declaration of Independence and the Constitution of the United States of America. The American government prints them by the millions. Inside was a cheque for twenty-five dollars made out to the Romanian Student League on a bank in Kentucky. The miner had never seen a cheque. He did not know what it was. He could not read English either. I tried to explain that the pamphlet now in my hand was a historical document and not usually considered inflammatory political material—though it was, of course, but that was too complicated to explain. He wanted to tell us about the drugs he found—four sacks of white powder in the university; a doctor from the ambulance said it was heroin. He knew: 'He is a doctor.'

At ten o'clock that morning I spotted two Americans, obviously tourists, approaching Victory Square, cameras hanging from their necks. That two tourists should be sightseeing this day in Bucharest was so bizarre it was ludicrous. What did they imagine they were seeing? Cameras were of course forbidden. Soldiers saw the cameras the same time Alec Russell and I did, and the terrified couple were dragged and pushed and carried behind the cordons of troops around the Foreign Ministry. Alec and I showed our credentials and were allowed through the first line of troops and then the second. An officer was shaking his fist at the couple, then let them go, but not before someone stomped on the man's foot. They walked quickly away. Alec and I ran after them, and just as I asked their names I was grabbed from behind and shoved behind a truck. They then grabbed Alec. We were trying to show our press passes to a major—and the beating started.

During it the major stood about three feet from us, screaming, shaking his fist. He had grabbed our credentials and Alec's notebook; fortunately I had stowed mine in a back pocket concealed by my jacket. Four soldiers and a couple of *Feseniști* ripped open my shirt. I was very angry. I had never been beaten up before. I remember every blow. There were six of them: a club in the left kidney, another on the shoulder, a vicious uppercut to the jaw that I could still feel a week later, a kick in the back, a club in the chest, a kick in the leg. I felt none of them then or felt them only through a kind of adrenalin rush. They tried to drag us behind another truck, farther out of sight from the street. I was more frightened now. I did not want to disappear behind a truck in Bucharest. I did not want to end up in a hospital in Bucharest. I wanted my credentials back, and these goons had ruined my shirt! One cooler head, I didn't know whose, prevailed and the men were persuaded to release us. The major shoved us off but kept our credentials. We walked away as quickly as possible. They were following us—I could hear their footsteps—but I knew that to turn and face them would be a serious mistake. To run would be worse. We kept walking, cursing. There were no taxis.

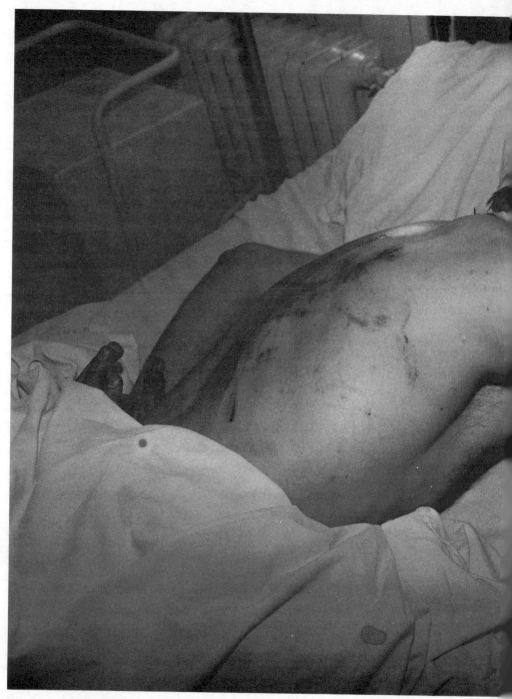

Miners' victim, Bucharest, June 14 1990.

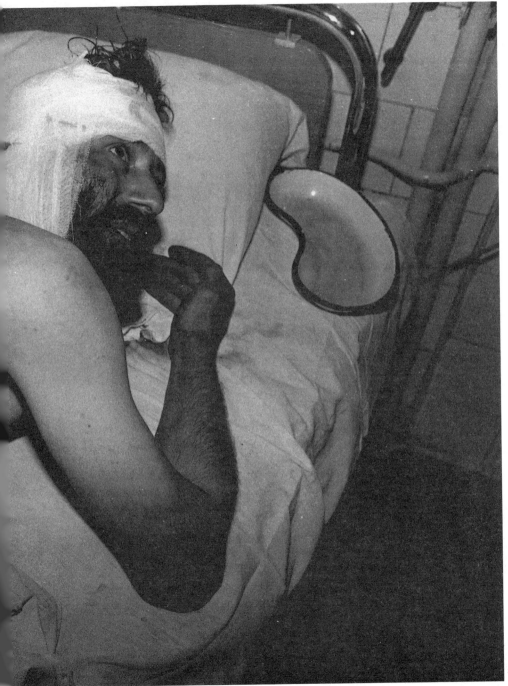

A tape has surfaced of a low-frequency police band radio, recorded on 13 June. The government has denounced it as a provocation, but it sounds convincing. The background noise, the sense of urgency, the confusion are all there, and it appears to confirm what many of us suspected: that the terrible violence and bloodshed that began that day, leading to the rampage of the miners on Thursday and Friday were deliberately provoked. On the tape, officer fifty-three says to officer fifty-two, 'Do you see any possibility of informing the president? We are starting to burn all of the buses. This was the agreement.' The recording implicates a Mr Magureanu. Virgil Magureanu is the head of the new Romanian Intelligence Service, whose purpose is 'to gather data and information on the activity of espionage and terrorist organizations against Romania, of extremists or of individuals who plan subversive actions to undermine the national economy, to destabilize the rule of law.' No one in Romania has seen the rule of law for some time; the rule of force and rumour and manipulation prevails. On the tape officer fifty-two says to officer fifty-three: 'I don't know how we can resolve this. Magureanu retreated and we don't know where he is. This was his business. . . The prime minister's orders were to keep order until the workers arrived.' Two people who have listened to the tape insist that one of the voices is that of the interior minister, General Chiţac, who has since been replaced. I did not recognize General Chiţac's voice, so I cannot say.

A few days later, Ion Iliescu was inaugurated President of Romania. The Athenaeum, where the ceremony took place, was ringed by troops and protected by tanks. I skipped it.

Two days later wreaths were laid in the University Square to the heroes of the Revolution. It has been six months since Ceauşescu fled. The Army band was playing the Romanian national anthem. The solemn tune floated up, on to my balcony and into my room at the Intercontinental where I was staying now, for safety reasons. I went to the balcony to watch. The church bells began to toll. All the church bells throughout

Photo: Chip Hires (Frank Spooner Pictures)

Miners in Bucharest, June 15 1990.

Romania were tolling at this hour. I cried. I could not help it.

Six days later I was packing to leave Romania for a time. My friend Sorin came by my room to say goodbye. I have a terrible memory for tunes and I asked him if he would sing for me the anthem '*Deşteoptăte romăne*'—'Romania, Awake!'

No, he said, he could not do it. He would write the words in my notebook. If he sang it he would cry. He wrote the words, but he cried anyway.

A couple of hours later I passed the Foreign Ministry on my way to the airport. Soldiers were still guarding it, but not as many as before. To the east of the building there was a long row of tanks.

17 December 1989: anti-government demonstrators massacred in Timişoara, during a protest against the *Securitate*'s attempt to deport Lászlo Tökes, an ethnic Hungarian pastor.

21 December: street fighting in Bucharest after a Ceauşescu rally turns into an anti-government demonstration.

22 December: Nicolae and Elena Ceauşescu flee from Bucharest.

23 December: the Ceauşescus are captured.

25 December: the Ceauşescus are executed.

26 December: the National Salvation Front name the new government, headed by President Ion Iliescu. The first non-communist political party in Romania since 1947 is re-established: the National Peasant Party.

27 January 1990: first local election is held in Timişoara.

28 January: opponents and supporters of the National Salvation Front clash in Bucharest.

22 April: full version of the trial of the Ceauşescus is shown on Romanian television for the first time. Students and others occupy University Square to remember those who died in the Revolution and protest against the presence of former Communists in the government.

20 May: the National Salvation Front wins a landslide victory in the election. Eighty-five per cent of votes go to the Front, giving them 325 of the 506 seats. There are 600 foreign observers, and allegations of electoral malpractice are made against the Front.

12 June: government deploys armed soldiers and police to quell a demonstration outside government headquarters. The demonstrators accuse the government of continuing the policies of Ceauşescu. The student anti-Front demonstration in University Square enters its seventh week.

13 June: police attempt to end the student occupation of University Square, arresting 263 protesters. At least five people killed in disturbances in Bucharest, which Iliescu describes as an attempted *coup* against the Front.

14 June: thousands of miners from the Valley of Jiu are brought to Bucharest in special trains at dawn.

15 June: Petre Roman, the prime minister, denies that the miners were acting on government orders. He does not condemn their behaviour despite international protest. Hospitals in Bucharest release statistics showing that 296 people have been treated for head injuries and broken bones. The opposition calls for the outside world to isolate the government.

16 June: troops and police patrol Bucharest. Iliescu claims to have averted a fascist *coup*. The European Community expresses 'shock and disappointment' at the miners' brutality.

20 June: Iliescu is formally inaugurated as president at a ceremony boycotted by the US ambassador, who announces that the US will now withhold all non-humanitarian aid from Romania.

14 July: defence minister General Stanculescu announces that former *Securitate* agents are to join the national guard service established after the June demonstrations.

ISABEL ELLSEN

CHILDREN'S SECTION,
GRADINARI HOUSE

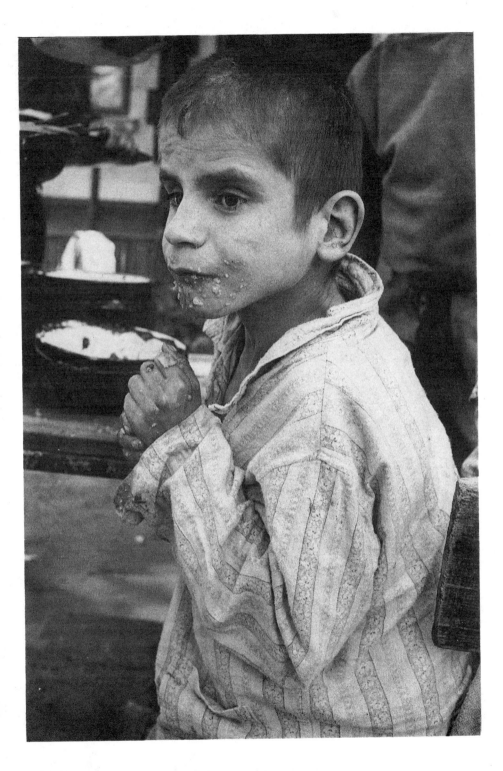

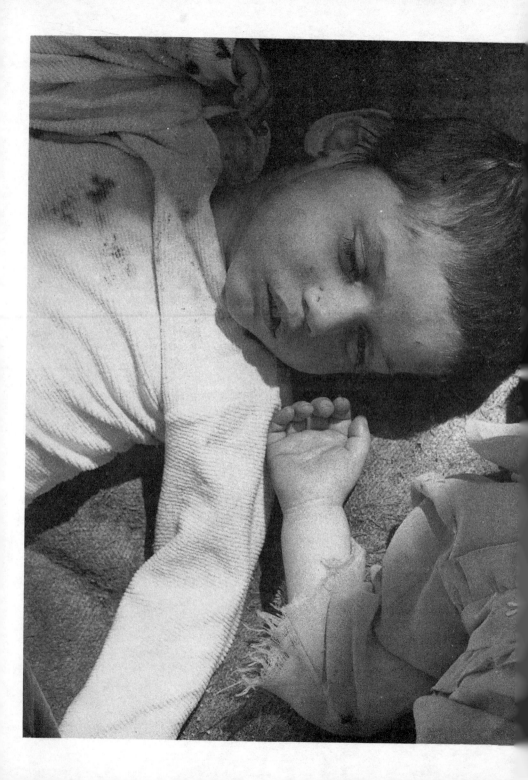

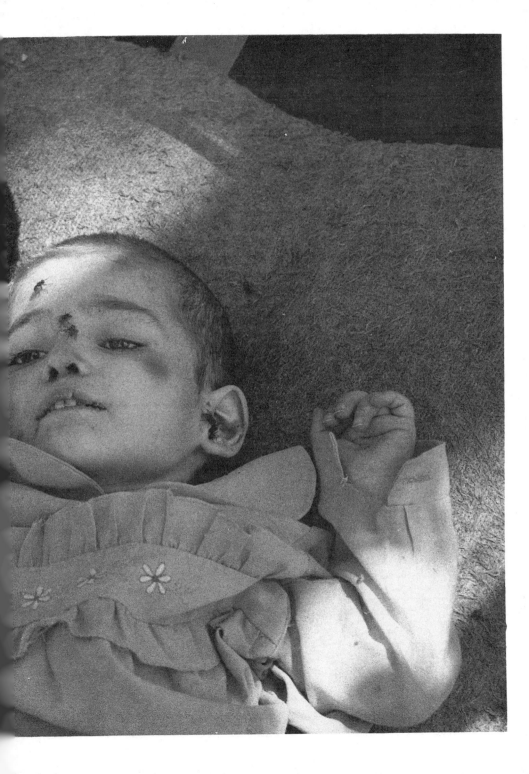

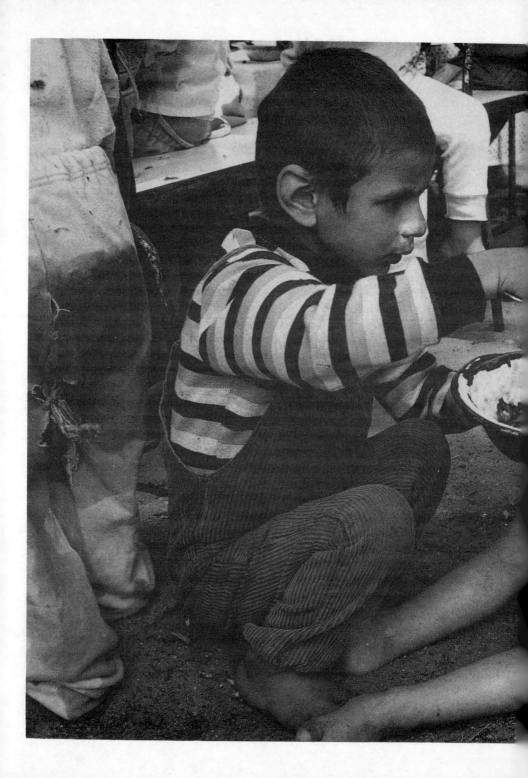

Gradinari House is thirty kilometres from Bucharest. One hundred and fifteen children live here. Some suffer from mental illness; others are orphans. The children range in age from fifteen months to sixteen years. During the day the children are left in the 'cages'; they sleep in them in the summer. Forty children died in Gradinari House last year. Officially, there are 800 houses like this in Romania.

Timothy Garton Ash
We The People

We The People is the eye-witness account, by one of Europe's most informed political observers, of one of Europe's most important political moments. As one communist regime fell after another in 1989, Timothy Garton Ash was there to witness the collapse.
He was in Warsaw when the government was humiliated by Solidarity in the elections. He was in Budapest, when Imre Nagy was finally given his proper burial. He was in Berlin, as the Wall opened. And he was in Prague with Václav Havel and the members of Civic Forum, as they made their 'Velvet Revolution'.

'It is with minimal exaggeration that I state that, in the future, there will probably be streets in Warsaw, Prague and Budapest bearing the name of Timothy Garton Ash.'
Karel Kyncl, *Independent*

Paperback £4.99 ISBN 0140 14023-9
Also available in paperback from Granta Books by
Timothy Garton Ash: *The Uses of Adversity, Essays on the Fate of Central Europe*, winner of the 1989 European Essay Prize.

GRANTA BOOKS

Martha Gellhorn
The View from the Ground

Martha Gellhorn's peacetime dispatches bear witness to six decades of change: America in the Great Depression, the betrayal of Czechoslovakia, Christmas with the unemployed in London, the trial of Adolf Eichmann, Spain in the days after Franco's death, Cuba revisited after forty-one years. Here is history as it looked and felt to the people who lived through it.

'An eloquent, unforgettable history of a chaotic century.'
San Francisco Chronicle

'Martha Gellhorn's writing is spiked with intelligence, individualism and moral indignation.'
New Statesman & Society

'Gellhorn's work is infused by passion as James Cameron said that all great reporting should be.'
Scotsman

'A sharp, eye, a retentive memory and a sparse, powerful prose.'
Sunday Telegraph

'Deep with humanity and beautifully written.'
Guardian

Hardback, 480 pages £14.95 ISBN 0140-14200-2
October paperback publication

VICTORIA TOKAREVA
DRY RUN

Ty address book is over-populated, like a communal
apartment during the post-war housing shortage. Several
pages have fallen out, and someone spilled water on one
page, smudging the ink. The whole book needs rewriting; at the
same time I must carry out a purge of the past: people should be
carried forward into the future, or buried in the vaults of memory.

Someone gave me a new address book as a present, so on this
fine day I am sitting down to transfer into it the names that I want to
keep. The old book is a cryptogram of my biography, coded in
letters, figures, names and telephone numbers. I regret parting with
it, but it has to be done, because time insists on forever recasting the
plot of my life.

I open the first page: 'A'. *Alexandrova, Mara . . .*

Her father was killed in the third year of the war. She and her
mother were evacuated to a Siberian village. Almost all she could
remember of those days as an evacuee was the large, coffee-
coloured rump of a horse seen through the window. The horse
belonged to the local policeman; he used to visit her mother, who
embroidered a shirt for him.

When the war ended, they returned to Leningrad. Mara went
to school, and in the school choir she used to sing:

Stalin—helmsman of our destiny,
Stalin—marching at our head!
With a joyful song of victory,
Our people follow Stalin's lead!

Her mother was busy with her own life. She was past thirty. At
that age a woman needs a husband, and not just any husband but
one she loves. He must be sought for, and the search is a serious
business, taking all a woman's time and energy.

Their home was overrun with rats. Her mother would catch
them with a rat-trap and then drown them by dropping the cage into
a bucket of water. Mara remembered the rats' paws and the five
wet, pink little fingers with which they gripped the wires, clambering
up the sides of the cage to escape from the inexorably rising water.
Her mother lacked the sense to spare her daughter this spectacle.

In school Mara was a solidly average pupil but she only ever
made friends with the bright ones. Proximity to the élite meant that

something of their glory rubbed off on her. This was a way to satisfy her power complex, though it must also be said that the bright pupils were glad to be friends with Mara and sometimes they threw scenes of jealousy in their rivalry for the privilege of commanding her devotion.

Stalin died in the spring of 1953. From morning to night the radio played sad but splendid funeral music. It was a good time, because school classes stopped almost completely. The teachers wept real tears. Together with her friend Rita Nosikova, Mara planned to go to Moscow for the leader's funeral, but her mother refused to give her the money for the fare . . .

At that age, time drags slowly but passes quickly. Mara grew and grew, and grew up. One evening at the Officers' Club she met Zhenya Smolin, a handsome journalist. He asked her to dance a waltz with him. They spun round the ballroom. Her dress flew out around her. With centrifugal force pulling them apart, they held each other tight with their young arms and never stopped looking into each other's eyes. It was deliriously exciting.

When Mara was eighteen, she married him.

It was an impetuous marriage, an express marriage. No sooner had they signed the book in the registry office than they started a furious quarrel and went on quarrelling morning, noon and night . . . They would fight passionately and then just as passionately make it up. Their life consisted of quarrels and love-making. It was a perpetual struggle for power. Mara discovered she was pregnant; she was not sure whether it was from quarrelling or embracing. After five months her belly had swollen but then it suddenly seemed to start shrinking. Apparently there are pregnancies that take a pathological turn, when the foetus, having developed to a certain stage, starts to retrogress, withers and perishes. In defending the mother from infection, nature destroys the foetus. It is born after nine months, apparently at full term, but tiny and dead and enveloped in its own sarcophagus. Such things happen. And it had to happen to Mara, of all people. The doctors tried to find the cause, but Mara knew: her love had started to wither and, without maturing to its proper, full growth, had begun to decay until it died.

After hospital, Mara went south in order to plunge into the salt, resilient sea and wash her past life out of herself, then to lie on the beach and close her eyes. Nobody was to touch her. She needed nothing.

She was in this state when the quiet, gentle, taciturn Dmitry Palatnikov found her and began silently to court her. She called him Dima. He was chronically silent but understood everything, like a dog; and, dog-like, he exuded devotion and warmth. People are silent for two reasons: either because they have a great intellect or because they are hopelessly stupid. Mara tried to make out which of these was the case with Dima. Sometimes he would utter a complete thought or make an observation. These were by no means stupid, though not always relevant. When Dima didn't like something he would shut his eyes: see no evil, hear no evil. Clearly this was a relic of childhood. When he opened them again, nothing in his expression had changed. He was the same whether his eyes were open or shut; they were inexpressive and in no way reflected the workings of his mind. Eyeless and wordless as he was, he alone of all people suited her shattered nerves and her desecrated body.

Mara and Dima went back to Leningrad together. Dima was a traditionalist: since they had made love, they had to marry. So they got married, joined a housing co-operative and bought a car.

Dima was a doctor—an ear, nose and throat specialist. Financially, though, the main load-bearing member of their household was Mara. She discovered that she had a talent: she could dressmake and she made a lot of money at it. Her prices were clearly not in keeping with the finished product and exceeded common sense. Her system, however, was based on the voluntary principle: if you don't want it, you don't pay. If you pay, it means you're a fool. Mara made her money out of people's foolishness.

There are always plenty of fools, and the money flowed in like a river. One thing was lacking: prestige. In those days, in the sixties, cosmonauts were fashionable. There weren't many of them and they were mostly to be seen in the media, like film stars. But a dressmaker was, by comparison, something archaic and unmodern, like a Chekhovian seamstress. If you said to someone 'dressmaker'—they would laugh. What's more, they would report you for illegal moonlighting. Mara asked all her customers not to give the number of her flat to the woman lift-operator, who sat downstairs; her unblinking stare bored into every visitor like a power-drill. Mara would stitch away and jump out of her skin every time the bell rang, like some political conspirator in an underground movement.

Nowadays much has changed. So many cosmonauts have been spawned that you can't keep count of them. And a talented dress-designer has a profile as high as any film star's. But that is today; then, it was different . . .

Tired of trembling at the sound of the doorbell, of feeling humbled and of piling up cash to acquire ever more goods and chattels, Mara set dressmaking aside and went to work in television. Now *there* is a job which depersonalizes you quite as much as the metro in the rush-hour; on the other hand, when someone asks you, 'What do you do?', you can reply, 'Director's assistant in TV'; it doesn't just sound better than 'dressmaker': there is no comparison, although in fact a TV director's assistant is little more than a waitress: gimme this, go for that, clear off.

It was at this stage of her life that I came across Mara and her name was first entered in my address book.

We met at Komarovo, a resort near Leningrad. My husband and I had been given a holiday voucher to spend in the rest-home owned by the Theatre Workers' Union. It was out of season, the place was empty, and the TWU was offering places to members of other, non-theatrical professional associations—including ours, the geologists'.

One day when my husband and I were out walking in the woods not far from the rest-home, we were approached by a young woman wearing an expensive, full-length fur coat who asked us whether we were staying at the TWU home. Hearing that we were, she began to ask what the place was like; whether she and her husband could see our room; and so on. I didn't want to go back indoors just then but it was impossible to refuse, because she was wearing a real fur coat and all I had on was some synthetic rubbish—but also because she *pressured* you. It was somehow implicit that I must obey her. I said humbly, 'But of course'—and led the unknown couple to our room, number 315. There she inspected everything, including the wardrobes and cupboards, which she opened unceremoniously. Meanwhile she introduced herself and her husband: her name was Mara and his was Dima.

Deadpan Dima stood around without a word, except to say occasionally: 'Come on, Mara, let's go . . .'
We went downstairs to see our visitors off. Dima walked alongside as if none of this was anything to do with him, but he exuded calm and decency. They were a well-assorted pair, like a variety double-act: the comic and the straight man. Dima said nothing, while Mara was permanently in top gear: her voice swooping up and down, she hooted with laughter; she flashed her handsome white teeth, shook her reddish-gold hair, asserting herself, her fur coat and her entire personality—she simply discharged megavolts of surplus energy into the cosmos. I guessed she had approached us on that path in the woods out of boredom. Bored at being alone with Dima, she needed an audience. The available audience at that moment happened to be me, a pathetic geologist living on my pay—ordinary, mass-produced, thirteen to the dozen.

They left that evening after dinner. Mara promised to make me a skirt, and in exchange she demanded my friendship. I agreed. There was some magnetic force in her: you didn't want to, but you did what she asked. It's like the habit of eating sunflower seeds and spitting out the husks: it's disgusting but you can't stop yourself.

When they had gone, I said, 'They've asked us over to their place.'

'Well, you can go without me,' said my husband curtly.

She repelled my husband; she attracted me. There was about her that degree of 'over'—over the top, overbearing, overstepping the mark, overdoing it—which has always enthralled me, enmeshed as I am in 'inconvenient', 'unacceptable', 'impossible' and 'it's not done.' I was something elemental and fresh, like Jewish matzo: good to eat with spicy food. For me, Mara became that spicy food.

Drawn by the idea of a custom-made skirt, the promised friendship and the need for a taste of some of Mara's 'over the top' quality, I called her up and went to Leningrad.

She opened the door to me. I shuddered as if someone had doused me in cold water. Mara was completely naked. Her breasts looked splendid but indecent, like two domes without crosses on a desecrated Russian church. I expected her to be embarrassed, that she would run off in search of a dressing-gown, but Mara stood there looking calm and even a touch arrogant, as though she were wearing an expensive evening gown.

'But . . . but . . . ' I could only stutter, 'you're . . . naked.'

'Well, so what?' Mara was surprised at my reaction. 'It's a body. Is yours any different?'

I had to admit that, in general terms, mine was the same. I submitted and stepped inside. Mara went ahead of me, her bare bottom retreating into the flat.

'Were you in the bath?' I said, guessing.

'I take air-baths. One's skin has to breathe.'

Mara sat down at her sewing-machine and went back to making my skirt. She had tied a rough cloth under her chin and knotted it on the top of her head, the way undertakers tie up the chin of a dead person.

'What is that for?' I asked.

'To stop a double chin from forming. I have to hold my head down while I'm sewing.'

Mara finished the job in forty minutes, threw me the skirt and named her price. It was ten roubles more than we had agreed. That is simply not done. I felt ashamed for her, then embarrassed, and could only give a slight nod—meaning OK, I agree. Having paid her, I realized that although I still had enough money for my ticket back to Moscow, there was now not enough for a sleeping berth. No doubt the train conductor would be rather surprised.

'You can sew in the zip-fastener yourself,' said Mara. 'I haven't got a black one at the moment.'

In other words, she was ripping me off an extra ten roubles for *not* sewing in the zip.

The air-bath session ended. Mara untied the strip of cloth from her face and threw on a Japanese dressing-gown embroidered with dragons. The gown was made of the thinnest shot silk, silver-grey, mother-of-pearl.

'Did you make it yourself?' I asked.

'Oh, come now—this is a genuine kimono.' Mara was offended. 'The real thing.'

I got the message: she made clothes for other people so that she could buy 'the real thing' with the money she earned.

With her jaw free, Mara could eat and talk properly. She made coffee and began telling me about her neighbours in the next-door flat, number fifty: Sasha and Sosha. Sasha was short for Alexander, Sosha for Sophia. Sosha was little, ash-blonde and colourless, as if she had been pulled out of a bath of hydrogen peroxide. But there was something about her. You wanted to hold her still with your eyes and keep on looking at her . . . Those pale northern women, like the flowers of the north, are much more fascinating than any of the blatantly gorgeous flowers that bloom in the south: these are striking to look at and can rock you back on your heels, but you don't stay looking at them for long. They're boring. Yet you can stare at a forget-me-not for ever, it draws you in . . . But the point of the conversation was not northern flowers or Sosha. The fact was that Mara had fallen in love with Sasha, and she needed to talk about it to someone, otherwise the tension was too much for her to bear alone.

Mara had chosen me to be that 'someone'. I was safe, I lived in another city, a superficial, passing acquaintance like a taxi-driver to whom one can pour out one's confession and then get out and instantly forget about it. Instead of saying goodbye and leaving at once, I stayed and sat there, hypnotized, until two o'clock in the morning. Meanwhile my dear husband was waiting for me on the platform at Komarovo station in the dark and cold, meeting train after train and not knowing what to think.

We spent the night sorting out Mara's love life and the next day catching up on our sleep. A whole twenty-four hours of my precious holiday had gone out of the window. And why? All because of Sasha and Sosha. Or rather, because of Mara. Later I discovered a new law of nature: where there was Mara, there was disaster. If she phoned, it would be at the moment when I was washing my hair. I would run dripping to the telephone and explain that I couldn't talk but somehow I would talk to her all the same; shampoo would trickle into my eyes, water down my back, and I would end up getting chilled and catching a cold. If Mara's phone-call came in

more normal circumstances and I would successfully replace the
receiver having dealt with her, then, as I walked away from the
telephone, I would catch my foot in the cord, fall and
simultaneously smash my kneecap and the telephone. Result: I
would be limping and cut off from the world, as though God were
shaking his finger under my nose and warning me not to speak to
that woman. But next time the devil would give me a wink and I
would be unable to resist her.

The stay at Komarovo ended with my husband and me
returning to Moscow on dusty couchettes, with a skirt without a zip,
the nasty aftertaste of a quarrel and a ruined holiday.

Mara remained in Leningrad, working in television and
moonlighting at home with her sewing-machine. Or
rather, the other way round. She was working with the
sewing-machine, while she did her job at the TV studios on the side,
for pin-money. But at home or at work, day or night, she thought
ceaselessly about Sasha. Dima was the same age as Sasha but there
was something *old* about him. At the age of three he was already an
elderly person. In their family album there is a photograph of him
aged three, with pendulous cheeks and a dignified expression—like
a dentist with a successful practice. On the other hand, Sasha, at
forty, might have been a three-year-old, as helpless and impractical
as a genius, everything about him crying out: love me . . . Lucky
Sosha.

One day, out of the blue, Dima became fascinated with
'alternative' medicine; he would save his urine in jars—supposedly
a new form of treatment: one put back into one's body its own
excretions. And right next door was Sasha, so clean after a swim, so
soulful after playing in a symphony by Kalinnikov, as different as an
alien from another planet . . . The best in life was passing Mara by;
all that she had was her trivial work in television, her fickle
customers and a row of three-litre jars full of piss.

One day when Mara came home, the lift-operator—she with
the gimlet stare—beckoned to Mara and informed her, as a great
secret, that the wife of the couple in number fifty had run off with
another man. This other man had driven up that morning in a yellow
Zhiguli; they had carried a rocking-chair together with Sosha's

clothes and bed-linen tied up in bundles. Her fancy man was dark and good-looking, with a moustache and a stylish line in dress: he wore trainers with letters printed on them and the same letters were on his zip-up jacket.

'Perhaps he wrote the letters there himself,' Mara suggested, as a ploy to distract the lift-woman from seeing her altered expression.

That evening, returning from a concert, wearing a black suit and a bow-tie, Sasha asked Mara how to wash potatoes: should they be washed before or after peeling them? Mara said, 'Twice—before and after.' Sasha stood there and did not go away. Mara invited him in. She fried some potatoes for him while Sasha sat in the kitchen alongside Dima, both silent. Dima was not a talkative person, while Sasha didn't want to talk to anyone yet hated being alone. This was just what he needed: to sit in silence with somebody, and not just anybody but a lively, intelligent and perceptive person.

Mara fried the potatoes in boiling fat, as they do in restaurants. There was no meat, but she fried cheese *suluguni*, a Georgian speciality, first dipping it in beaten egg and flour, and with these she fed the two men. It was the first time in his life that Sasha had eaten hot cheese. He ate and wept, though the tears did not flow from his eyes but filled his heart. Mara loved Sasha, so her heart grew heavy with Sasha's tears. She said nothing.

That was at eleven o'clock at night. At four in the morning Mara slipped out of the broad marital bed, away from the sleeping, snorting Dima, pushed her feet into slippers, put on the dragon kimono, went out on to the landing and rang Sasha's doorbell.

Footsteps were heard immediately; Sasha was not asleep. The door was flung open without preliminaries. Sasha had not locked or bolted it. Mara saw the needle on the dial of Sasha's features register all his feelings: from one hundred degrees of delirious happiness it fell first to perplexity, then to zero and further downward to several degrees minus. It was all quite clear to Mara: Sasha had been expecting Sosha, believing that she would change her mind and come back.

'Forgive me,' she said apologetically, 'but I was frightened. I had a feeling you were going to throw yourself out of the window. Nonsense, of course . . . Do forgive me . . .'

'Come in,' Sasha invited her.

'But it's late,' Mara objected feebly.

'Rather it's early,' Sasha corrected her and went to make coffee. What else does one do for an unexpected female visitor at four o'clock in the morning?

Mara sat down at the table, looked at Sasha's back and felt guilty. What for? Because she loved him and he didn't love her. She had just read this on Sasha's face. In what way was she any worse than Sosha, that colourless moth, that traitress? That was why she was worse than Sosha: one should make men suffer, and not wag one's tail at them. Mara no longer recognized herself. She, in principle, had been designed and built by nature as a consumer. She was prone to consume everything, moveable and immovable, to cram it into herself through every orifice: eyes, ears, mouth and so on. Yet now, with this man, all that was reversed; she wanted to share everything with him, to sacrifice her last crust for him, give him her last shirt; simply to make him a gift of herself, body and soul—if only he would have her. If only she could be of use to him. It was clear that so many unexpended emotions, words, endearments, so much insight and energy had been accumulating inside Mara that they had formed there into a deep, fertile layer of spiritual humus. A grain of seed only had to fall on this rich soil, and at once—like in an animated cartoon—the magic plant of love would instantly spring forth, full-grown.

Mara felt an inward chill and she longed to complain. But to whom? One needs to complain to someone who is interested in you. Her mother, for example. But her mother had forgotten how she herself had once suffered; now her only response to life's problems was mockery. Complain to Dima? But what could she say to him? That she loved their neighbour, Sasha, that she only lived with Dima out of fear of loneliness? So who does Mara complain to? Who do you think?

Mara gave in and stopped being like a sergeant-major. Sasha poured out the coffee, sat down beside her, laid his head on her shoulder and said, 'Mara, do you know a good doctor? Find me a doctor.'

'What's the matter with you?'

'I . . . well, the fact is, I'm not a man.'

'In what sense?' Mara did not understand.

'In the direct sense. That's why Sosha left me.'

'But perhaps the trouble lies with Sosha, not you.'

Mara sensed people through her skin. She was convinced that sexual energy, like any other, has density and a detectible radius of effect. Some men give off absolutely nothing at all. Zero. With others, you have to put on a lead-lined suit if you don't want to get scorched. She could feel Sasha's sexual aura even through the concrete walls of his flat.

'What's Sosha got to do with it?' Sasha raised his head from her shoulder. 'I don't think you understand what I'm talking about.'

'I understand very well. Come, let's go.' Mara stood up from the table.

'Where to?' Sasha asked, puzzled.

'I'll show you.'

Sasha obeyed and followed Mara. They lay down on the wide Arab bed. Having cast doubt on Sosha, Mara began to demonstrate what Sosha *should* have been doing. And proved it brilliantly. She proved to Sasha not only his male prowess but more—that he had a genius for sex; that he belonged to the caste of the élite. Only those with a phenomenal charge of the life-force can sense it and respond to it, its concentrated essence, with such finesse and such power. There were no more men like Sasha. Well, perhaps there might be one other, somewhere in India or in China. But there were certainly none in the Soviet Union. At any rate she, Mara, had never heard of them.

Sasha smiled blissfully, exhausted but buoyant. Mara raised herself on one elbow and looked at him. He was as much *hers* as though he had grown within her, as though she had given birth to him and until now they had shared a common bloodstream.

'Would you like me to tell you how much I love you?' Mara asked.

He gave a barely perceptible nod. He lacked the strength to nod more deeply. Mara sought the words for a long time, but only the simplest, most banal words would come to her.

'You're good,' she said. 'You're better than all the others. You're unique.'

Sasha wanted to sleep, but it was a pity to waste time on sleep.

They talked until six o'clock in the morning.

In the early morning Mara returned to the sleeping, all unsuspecting Dima. But Sasha couldn't sleep. He had started a new life.

That evening he played a concert. The conductor of the orchestra he played in said that Sasha's D-flat had made the entire symphony. His colleagues in the orchestra noticed that sparks were flashing in his eyes, like a firework display on the First of May. He had grown younger, fitter and better-looking. Sasha, in his turn, became keenly aware of the remarkable talents around him, breathing inspiration into all those bits of metal and pieces of wood. After all, what is a trombone or a violin? Metal piping and a few sticks of wood; but when a man breathes his soul into them they come alive. And vice versa. If you extinguish a man's soul, he becomes a piece of wood or a lump of metal. It happens.

After the concert, Sasha didn't simply walk or stroll home as before—he cut a path through space. He rushed home. There, Mara was waiting for him. She had discovered Sasha, as though he were a new continent, and she intended to plant her flag and found her state on that continent.

Sasha, however, was not looking so far ahead. He was simply rejoicing, reaffirming his personality. Reaffirming and confirming.

A month passed.

During that month Sosha was nest-building with her new man Irakly. It is one thing to find someone but another matter to live with them. Irakly filled the flat with guests, which was all a part of Georgian tradition, while Sosha silently served them at table and cleared away after them. That was also part of national tradition: a woman had to know her place.

Irakly was a civil engineer and was writing a dissertation on the topic of 'Eliminating the Consequences of a Nuclear Explosion'. Sosha was under the impression that after a nuclear explosion there wouldn't be anyone left to eliminate the consequences. She understood nothing about it and didn't want to, though on television they went on droning away about it from morning till night and about how terrible life would be. Yet Sosha had understood everything about Sasha's music. In the seven years of their life together she had learned to read a conductor's score, to distinguish the principal from the subsidiary parts, knew all the players in the orchestra and had learned how they blend their voices. With her eyes closed she could tell: that's Dima playing . . . that's David . . . that's Andrei . . . and now they're all playing together: Dima, David and Andrei.

Sosha would recall her former life with nostalgia, although she was perfectly happy with Irakly. She cooked him Georgian *khinkali* instead of Russian *pelmeny* and as she did so would reflect that Sasha was abandoned and hungry, whereas Irakly was surrounded by guests, *khinkali* and Sosha. She took to phoning Sasha's number but when she heard his voice she put down the receiver. What could she say to him?

Then one day Sasha said anxiously to Mara, 'Look, you'd better remove your hairpins, brooches and what not. Sosha's coming today.'

'What for?' Mara was unpleasantly surprised.

'She wants to cook lunch for me. She thinks I'm starving.'

Mara collected her bits and pieces and took them next door to Dima. She was living in two homes at once, thanks to the fact that her second home was only four paces away from the first.

Dima suspected nothing. He was busy. People were flocking to see him, since cranks and quacks have always been more trusted than proper doctors. It actually suited him when Mara spent time with the neighbours.

Sasha, too, liked the arrangement: his work was a pleasure, Mara was a pleasure. But the greatest pleasure of all were Sosha's visits. She would arrive at midday looking guilty and would move quietly about, tidying, cooking and vacuuming. Sosha was a good person. Mara was pure passion; he desired her. But he loved Sosha. It turned out that these were not one and the same thing. A clever man once said that the flesh was a horse and the spirit was a rider, and that if you only listened to the horse, you would end up living in a stable. You should obey the rider.

Mara removed her hairpins the first time and the second; but the third time she left them in the most conspicuous place. Sosha did not notice them. Then Mara phoned her at the scientific research institute where Sosha worked and suggested that they meet in the Tauride Gardens.

Mara was late. Sosha looked miserably at the palace which Potyomkin had built in which to receive Catherine the Great. But by then Catherine had another lover; she had had enough of Potyomkin. Why could Catherine do what she, Sosha, could not? Mara arrived, saying as she approached, 'Don't come and see Sasha any longer. You left him, and that's an end to it.'

'What business is it of yours?' Sosha asked in amazement.

'It's very much my business. He's mine.' (Sosha's eyes almost popped out of her head.) 'Yes, mine,' Mara insisted. 'Body and soul. And you mustn't have anything more to do with him. We can manage without you making mucky little bowls of soup for him.'

Dima had worked out that when cows are pole-axed in the slaughterhouse they experience mortal fear; that fear produces hormones which enter the bovine bloodstream and pass from the bloodstream into the muscles. Thus every single human meat-eater becomes poisoned with the secretions of another creature's fear . . . Hence aggression, crime, illness and premature ageing. We should instead eat the fruits of the sea and the forest; feeding ourselves on the flesh of other living, rational beings is tantamount to eating our own kind.

Sosha was not disconcerted by the 'mucky little bowls of soup' but by Sasha's double-dealing. He was like Janus—two-faced. Well, so what. At least everything was clear now. No need to feel pangs of conscience or torment herself any longer. She could just get divorced without any fuss and remarry in the normal way. And give Sasha to Mara.

'So much for you!' Sosha held up two of her pale, slender, well-bred fingers at Mara in the form of a 'V'.

'He's mine!' Mara repeated, ignoring the two-figured salute. 'We shall see . . .'

That same evening Mara rang the bell of their flat. Sosha opened the door. She was wearing an apron. Evidently her Georgian had trained her to work round the clock.

'I left a malachite ring here,' said Mara.

'Where?' Sosha asked.

'In the kitchen. Or it may have been in the bedroom.' Mara stressed the places she was wont to inhabit.

Sosha did not invite her in. She went away and came back again.

'There's no such ring,' she said. 'You must have left it in someone else's bedroom.'

And she shut the door.

A week later Sasha walked into the open lift. Mara was in it. Had he known she was there, he would have walked up the stairs to the sixteenth floor. They rode up together in silence. Sasha tried to look past her, but Mara insisted on staring directly at him, trying to catch his eye. Then she asked, also directly, 'Is this how you always behave?'

'I suppose so,' Sasha replied.

That was all.

Six months later Sosha went back to Irakly. Mara made no attempt to find out the reason. She did not go back to Sasha. Nor did he ask her to. He was hoping to find a woman who would combine flesh and spirit in one, where horse and rider would think alike and move together in one direction.

Mara's life as a shuttle came to an end. She settled down, ensconced herself quietly alongside Dima and told everyone she was fine. That the family was the laboratory of social stability, and her home was her castle. She invented the remark about the laboratory; the English had already coined the phrase about the castle. Sometimes, though, for no apparent reason Mara in her castle would throw a fit of hysterics, when she would hurl crockery out of the window. Dima was horrified, in case the cups and plates might hit someone on the head.

Against the background of people's private lives, the political life of the country flowed on. Nikita Sergeyevich Khrushchev came to power, and his first act was to disavow Stalin. Stalin, 'helmsman of our destiny', Stalin, 'marching at our head!', turned out to have been a tyrant and a murderer. The Thaw touched everyone with its breath of spring. Solzhenitsyn's *One Day in the Life of Ivan Denisovich* was published; everyone read it and realized that times had changed.

Nikita Sergeyevich was human; there was no need to fear him, and one could even tease him by calling him 'corn-cob'. It all ended with him being thrown out of his job. He was the first and so far the only head of the state to have been dismissed while still alive and allowed to die as a pensioner. The sculptor whom Khrushchev had publicly insulted carved a memorial gravestone for him made from black and white stones conjoined. Light and shade. Tragedy and farce.

From 1965 began the time now designated the era of stagnation. A new term—'dissident'—made its appearance, together with its derivatives: 'He's started dissidenting,' 'a dissidentary occupation' and so on. The stagnation was evident in politics and in the economy, but in Mara's life the seventies was a period of storm and stress.

Mara met Myrzik. He had a real name and surname and a profession: film cameraman's assistant. But she called him simply Myrzik, and it stuck.

They met at the television studio. One day as they were leaving together, Mara complained that television ate up all one's time, leaving nothing over for any kind of personal life.

'How old are you?' Myrzik asked in surprise.

'Thirty-seven,' Mara replied.

'But what sort of personal life can you expect to have at thirty-seven?' said Myrzik, sincerely amazed. 'It's all over. The train's gone, and they've pulled up the rails.'

Mara looked in astonishment at this idiot, a visitor from Moscow sent to Leningrad on an assignment. He in turn looked Mara up and down with the blatant stare of a one-time orphanage child.

Later they both recalled that this look had decided everything.

Was it love at first, or rather at second, sight? It was both more complicated and simpler than that.

Her life with Dima had come to an end. She had died there and she had to get away from it. Mara even thought of finding a worthwhile Jew and emigrating with him over the deep blue sea, as far away from home as possible. But no worthwhile Jew turned up. Myrzik turned up. Mara realized that he was on the young side for her and a bit scraggy but she had to put an end to her old life and start again from scratch.

When Mara announced to Dima that she was in love, Dima did not grasp what she wanted from him.

'I love him,' Mara explained.

'Well, go ahead and love him. Who's stopping you?'

'I want to leave you.'

'What for?'

'So that I can love him.'

'I won't stand in your way.'

Mara lowered her head. At that moment she felt that Dima was bigger and better than Myrzik, who wanted her all to himself, exclusively, whereas Dima, if he couldn't give her everything she wanted, was ready to step aside and care for her from a certain distance. She, Mara, was trying to thrust him out of her orbit. And he was afraid, not for himself but for her.

Mara burst into tears.

The conversation took place in a café. Myrzik was sitting at a nearby table, like a stranger. From his position he was watching to see that Dima didn't take Mara away; that there were no hitches; that it should end with him, Myrzik, as the winner.

Later he said to Mara, 'Your head was lolling, like a wounded bird's. I felt terribly sorry for you.'

Mara wondered where he had ever seen a wounded bird. No doubt he had knocked one down himself. Orphanage kid, after all.

Mara and Myrzik moved to Moscow. Having settled in the capital, Mara turned up at our flat and brought Myrzik with her. She took him around with her everywhere she went, as proof of her power as a woman, a kind of living medal. Myrzik adored Mara. Everything she said or did struck him as pure genius; he couldn't stop looking at her.

My husband and I had just had a daughter and we felt we had done the only right and proper thing. But when Mara's and Myrzik's happiness flared up in front of us, my life, draped in dirty nappies, suddenly seemed colourless. We were sitting in the kitchen, drinking tea. Mara was showing Myrzik off to us.

'Look at this hand.' She grabbed his wrist and pulled the hand forward for inspection. It was just a hand like any other, but Mara roared with laughter, her large bright teeth flashing. 'Look at this ear.' She started pushing aside his blond, Yesenin-like, curly hair. Myrzik struggled free from her fingers. Mara burst out laughing.

They both radiated happiness. Myrzik's happiness was sunny, Mara's lunar—a reflection of his. But it was still happiness.

Suddenly Mara yanked Myrzik out of his chair and they started to leave for home. Our baby was asleep. We saw them off a short way down the street. Mara led me on ahead and began trying to persuade me to leave my husband: it was so good when you left your husband, she insisted.

As I listened to Mara I thought about my own love. I had met my husband on a geological expedition; we were both free, and things took their natural course. We were sleeping in four-man tents so at night we went out into the forest and spent a long time finding a spot that wasn't marshy and where there were no ants. We finally discovered a smooth, firm patch and spread out a waterproof cape—only to be immediately lit up by the headlights of a lorry. It turned out we were planning to make love in the road. I sprang into the bushes like a mountain goat, losing my bra as I did so. Next morning some fellow geologists from our party found us, but they didn't give us away. Later, when I was chairing a Komsomol meeting and calling upon them to observe the Komsomol code of honesty and a clean conscience, the boys in the back row sneakily held up my bra and waved it at me.

It was a good time, but it passed. After ten years our love had wearied and become a bit routine, like putting on one's working clothes. Yet I knew that I would never start a new life and I envisaged my future as stretching out far ahead, as level and monotonous as the steppes.

No doubt my husband was thinking the same. We walked back home in silence, like strangers. Our baby woke up and cried. I had the feeling that Mara burned, gave light, smoked and dripped wax . . . She stirred longings in me for fateful passions, for the hot breath of life. But what would they bring?

So Mara and Myrzik were in Moscow. More exactly, in Myrzik's one-room flat in Bibirevo, a dormitory suburb almost as near to Kaluga as to Moscow, where the rows of identical blocks of flats are as depressing as a wet summer.

Mara called in a joiner called Gena, who lined the bare balcony with wood, insulated the walls and ceiling and put in central heating. The result was another room, long and narrow, like a section of corridor, but still it was an extra room. Mara set up a table there, on it her Singer sewing-machine, and an ironing-board along the wall. And so—forward . . . As a way of life, it was familiar and enjoyable; she only made dresses for people she liked, physically and spiritually. She flung herself into friendships of such intensity and closeness that there wasn't even room to push a piece of paper between Mara and her friend, but then she would equally suddenly quarrel and reject them. She had a need for conflict. A diabolical spirit always lurked inside her and would lash out; fate had endowed her with a non-returnable ticket to hell.

A year later Mara exchanged Bibirevo for Kutuzovsky Prospect in central Moscow, bought a second-hand Moskvich car and a Japanese Seika camera. The camera was intended for Myrzik. Mara had decided to make him into a press photographer who would catch the fleeting moment—beautiful or ugly, depending on what the public wanted at a given time: a burning lorry; a record-breaking worker; the first day at school.

In the new flat Mara knocked down a wall and had a dark-room built. She not only helped Myrzik to develop his prints but to select their subject-matter. She turned out to have a talent for this, as she had for so many things. Myrzik was invited to work for Novosti Press Agency, taking pictures extolling the Soviet way of life for propaganda abroad. Mara saw to it that he had a one-man exhibition of his work, then saw to it that he had blazing rows with everybody. Myrzik was sacked from his job.

Mara was like a strong medicine with side-effects. On the one hand it cures; on the other it induces weakness and nausea. At first Myrzik thought there was no alternative to this way of life, but one day he suddenly realized that there was: he left Mara and went to live with another woman, young and tenderly affectionate. He had made her pregnant and for her he was not Myrzik but Leonid Nikolayevich. With Mara he had forgotten his real name.

If one went back to the starting-point of their affair, then his feelings for Mara had been incomparably stronger and brighter than this new love. To live with Mara was to be without prospects. OK, there might be another car, a dacha in the country, a greenhouse at the dacha. But what for? Myrzik was bored with living for Mara and himself alone. He wanted a son, whom he could endow with a happy childhood. Brought up in an orphanage, Myrzik knew all about childhood.

Mara tried to stop Myrzik by threatening his material prosperity, but Myrzik craftily eluded her grasp. How he managed it is a mystery. He hung on to the Seika and chased her out of the flat, like a fox expelling a hare. That was Myrzik for you.

He went back to work and conquered the world. Well, not the whole world, but only that part of it that his mind could perceive. Myrzik did *not* come to grief without Mara, in fact he prospered— and that was most galling of all.

At that moment of crisis in her life Mara turned up at our flat and stayed with us for several days. She had—literally— nowhere to lay her head. Half the people in Moscow were acquaintances of hers, yet nobody needed her. They needed her when she was winning, when she was on the crest of the wave, but they did not need this woman who had been robbed and evicted. And she in her turn now had no need of the people who featured on the covers of magazines: she wanted to come and lean against us, ordinary and stable. We were geologists, people of the solid earth; we would not slide away from under her feet.

My husband went to spend the night with his parents, who lived on the floor below us. Mara slept on his side of the bed. Tragedy is said to ennoble people, but Mara managed to remain her old self. She stuck a clove of garlic up each nostril—she had a cold, and garlic has antiseptic properties—and because her nose was blocked up, she snored all night. These unfamiliar sounds and smells kept me awake. I finally fell asleep early in the morning, but at that moment Mara woke up, needing sympathy, and only a waking person is capable of displaying sympathy.

Mara shook me awake and informed me of all she had sacrificed for Myrzik's sake: Dima; her flat; the architecture of Leningrad . . . She invited me to remember what Myrzik had been when she had met him—a 'gopher': go for this, go for that, clear off. And what had he become? . . . And as soon as he had become something, he found he no longer needed people who knew where he had come from. What a fool she had been to trust him—after all, his character was written all over his face. He had used her, squeezed her out like a lemon and thrown her away. Alone, in a strange city.

'Go back to Leningrad,' I advised. 'Dima will be glad.'

Mara said nothing. She was thinking it over.

Could she go back to the sixteenth floor, where the yellow-eyed Sasha lived, so near that one only had to stretch out one's hand to him—and yet so far? . . . Like someone from another age. From the twenty-first century. Ah, Sasha, Sasha, twinkling star, how I wonder where you are! In the past, she would never have dreamt of abandoning spouse, home, possessions. But after Sasha, she had thrown them all to the winds without regrets. Myrzik—so what? She had survived Myrzik; though he, too, had turned out to be a powerful medicine with side-effects. He had cured her, but also crippled her. What a fate to suffer: she had made one of them into a man, the other into a press photographer. And what was her reward?

'Why should it always be the future that's happy, and not the present?' Mara asked. 'When society has got nothing to offer today, it offers you pie in the sky. And you've been taken in by it.'

So my generation had been conned. And the older generation, who believed in Stalin—what about them?

'You should emigrate,' I advised her, 'over there, they're all like you.'

It occurred to me that by the time she was forty she had already twice created a happy present for herself: with Dima in Leningrad and with Myrzik in Moscow. And my husband and I had been unable to allow ourselves to have a child for five years, because we had no home of our own. We had lived hugger-mugger with his parents. Now we would have to wait another ten years in order to move from a one-room into a two-room flat. No one can begin to live half-way decently until they're getting on for fifty, and at fifty-five they retire you on a pension. Work it out for yourself . . .

Mara disappeared to the Crimea. The sea had always been her salvation. She wiped away her tears with sea-water, went far away to where she could sunbathe naked, lying like a lizard on a stone and letting her bitten-off tail grow again.

At forty, a woman wants something strong that *she* can lean against. What sort of a man is firmly in the driving seat nowadays? Some Comrade Bigboss in a state enterprise, who gives orders, signs papers and puts the fear of God into his underlings. But how to find him? You can't just walk into Comrade Bigboss's office. You have to be issued with a pass. And then a policeman will compare that pass with your ID card and learn your data by heart: serial number, residence permit number, date of issue, issuing authority. You might go in and take a pot-shot at Comrade Bigboss, although Moscow isn't mafia-ridden Italy. Comrade Bigboss is pushing seventy, and who needs him? His blood has already curdled in his veins, like cottage cheese.

Mara, however, had already marked out her target and set herself on course to hit it fair and square, like a long-range ballistic missile. Having absorbed plenty of sun and restored her bitten-off tail to its full size, Mara went back to Moscow and wrenched Myrzik's Seika from his neck, almost pulling his head off in the process. She acquired the necessary piece of paper and entered Comrade Bigboss's office.

He already knew that someone was coming to take his photograph.

Mara sat down in front of him, legs crossed, and began to study his face. Comrade Bigboss was an elderly, wraith-like desiccated grasshopper, with eyes magnified by his thick spectacles. On his back, there was a protuberance under his jacket—perhaps it was a hump, perhaps a rubber oxygen bottle or perhaps a device for flying. His face was abstract, expressionless.

'Could you perhaps take off your glasses?' Mara inquired.

Mara trained Bigboss into getting used to her, and in a very short while it seemed to him that she had always been there. A woman gets the same feeling about the baby she is breast-feeding. It seems strange that only very recently the child wasn't there. At all. Anywhere. But once the infant is born, it seems he or she has been there for ever.

There was one great drawback to Bigboss: his age. And a further complication—one could only be indifferent to him. With her magnetic storm Mara drove indifference away, just as the clouds disperse on the opening day of the Olympic Games. Bigboss took energetic action, and within four months Mara was living in her own two-room flat in an elegant building in a quiet part of central Moscow, where Comrade Bigboss was as welcome as in his own home.

Mara could not stand dirt, so she always met him at the lift with his house-slippers and helped him to put them on. Then she put Bigboss into the bath, soaking and washing away his whole day and his whole previous life. Bigboss lay in the gentle foam and thought to himself: *this* is happiness. In his seventieth year. The only cloud in the sky was the thought of death. It would be hard to part from a life like this, which had so unexpectedly come to him in his declining years. But he tried not to think about it. As Napoleon's mother used to say, 'May it last as long as possible': meaning her son's reign as Emperor. Even so, she knitted him some woollen socks in case he should end up on the island of St Helena.

After the bath they would sit down to table. The table was of Karelian birch, the plates were blue-and-white English china, and on the china were steamed cutlets of minced veal, made in a mixer with the addition of cream. In the crystal glass was beetroot juice spiked with lemon. Beetroot cleanses the blood and drives out carcinogens. And there was Mara herself—in her dragon kimono, like a Japanese geisha. The Japanese understand the art of living. Dinner. Then the tea ceremony. Then another kind of ceremony.

So at the very end of his life Comrade Bigboss had acquired a second home and a mistress. His wife was a politician for whom the political had always been more important than the personal; the household was run by the maid, Valya, a wily peasant woman. His son was fifty and himself a grandfather. As an escape from loneliness, Bigboss worked from morning to night, serving the country in the sector entrusted to him. And suddenly—Mara. She became no less important to him than the whole Soviet Union. Sometimes even more important.

Mara, in return, was grateful to Bigboss. Gratitude makes for good soil, in which perhaps not the magic flower of love but a perfectly good tree may grow and bear edible fruit.

Mara's talents, it transpired, included not only dressmaking and photography but also affairs of state. She was something like a Marquise de Pompadour. And she pompadoured.

Her previous lovers, Sasha and Myrzik, had been Mara's creations.

She had moulded them, made them—admittedly for her own ends; she had created them and used them. But then, they had gained a lot too. Sasha had been fortified in spirit, flesh and hope; Myrzik in skill and money. But Comrade Bigboss was now doing the creative job on her. As a creator Mara was having a rest period, as a consumer she was triumphant. Bigboss could be consumed in handfuls; there was no longer any need to go out hunting.

Mara felt the need for some independent social activity. She had once acquired an external diploma in teaching. So Bigboss fixed Mara up with a place in a postgraduate institute attached to the Academy of Pedagogical Sciences. Mara began writing a dissertation, with the aim of becoming head of a department and then—who knows?—boss of the whole institute. And maybe, indeed, of the whole Academy. Why not?

At weekends Comrade Bigboss would go out to a dacha in the country with his family. This gave Mara some pauses in her life and, in her very next pause, Mara invited me to dinner—to show off her new power. She wanted to see me walking around her flat, dazzled by it all.

What amazed me most of all were the wide corridors and the light-fittings hanging from the ceilings and fixed to the walls. They seemed to have come from the Tauride Palace. Potyomkin had installed them, and Mara had removed them to this place, since she was now the present-day empress.

The candelabra gave off the dull glow of bronze, exuding an air of antiquity, mystery and the talent of an unknown master-craftsman. This was the rich home of an expensive kept woman.

I remembered my own flat, where the ceiling and the floor were just two and half metres apart, almost touching one's head; I used to call our flat a dug-out. All it needed was an old wind-up gramophone playing one of the wartime popular songs. I also recalled the home of my husband's parents: young communists of the 1920s, they had built this society selflessly and at much personal sacrifice—and where did they live? In one room in a shared flat, separated from their neighbours by a plywood partition. And they did not complain. They knew that Moscow was being strangled by a shortage of housing. People living in cellars had not yet been rehoused. Therefore they would put up with it. They would wait. Yet Mara had acquired all this at a stroke, simply because she had flashed her suntan at the right moment. In other words, for most people it was always the future that was going to be bright; for a few others there was a bright present.

Mara saw me looking depressed and decided it was because I envied her; that I, too, would like to be a Marquise de Pompadour at the court of a latter-day Louis.

'You know what you lack?' Mara said sympathetically.

'What?'

Mara sought for the right word, but there was only one. There were no analogies.

'You're very decent and respectable,' Mara's phrasing carefully avoided that word.

'It suits me that way,' I said.

'It suits you, because you hide behind decency and respectability to conceal your lack of initiative in life.'

'On the other hand, I do nobody any harm.'

'No harm—and no good either. You don't exist.'

This took my breath away. Mara interpreted my pause as a full stop and decided that the subject was exhausted. She moved on to the next one.

'My dissertation is almost finished. Soon I shall submit it to the examiners.'

My husband had spent six years fighting to complete his dissertation, a task akin to struggling through barbed wire.

'What's the topic?' I inquired, hiding my true feelings behind a show of interest.

'The sexual education of senior school pupils.'

I was reduced to a respectful silence. On that subject Mara was indeed a specialist, and there was no reason why she shouldn't pass on her experience to the rising generation.

Mara announced that she was working on the chapter entitled 'The Cultivation of Intercourse'—not *sexual* intercourse, naturally, but in the more general sense of social intercourse. No such subject is ever taught in schools; they rely on the family. But the family doesn't teach it either. People are devoid of good manners. Mara was collating and comparing the experience of other countries and religions. Her account of it was very interesting, and I was distracted from my mood of corrosive resentment at the class differences that existed in our supposedly classless society. Hypnotic waves emanated from Mara and transfixed me. Like a fish, I swam towards her baited hook.

Without the slightest sign that she was changing the subject, Mara asked me, 'Would you like to exchange your flat? For one with two rooms? There are three of you now, after all.'

I was struck dumb. It was my dream. The space I longed for. Happiness—not in the future but here and now.

'Could I?' I enquired, made timid by the mere hope.

'He's in Peru at the moment,' said Mara, meaning Comrade Bigboss. 'He'll be back in a week, and I'll have a word with him.'

Thus the bait was swallowed. Hook and all. Mara could now tug at my lip and pull me in any direction she liked. Which she did.

During the following week, Mara came to see me at home several times. She practically cleaned out my library. Library is perhaps too strong a word, but my husband and I did have a collection of our favourite books.

Apart from moral values, Mara also took away peace from our home. My husband hated her; he became nervous and reserved. Mara seemed not to notice this and rushed to kiss him every time. He would stiffen, awaiting her embrace with as much disgust as if he were being attacked by a crocodile—slippery, loathsome and dangerous. He didn't believe in the success of this project for a second and despised me for falling in with it. I was afraid that Mara would notice this, and the whole thing would collapse. What she needed was the devoted gaze of a dog, not the eye of a wolf, which, feed it as one may, keeps looking back at the woods. I arranged to take Mara out of doors. We were living on the very edge of Moscow, near a lovely stretch of primeval forest.

Spring was in full flood. Standing by itself near the path into the forest was a slender willow tree. Its buds were a gentle yellow, fluffy, as big as chicks. The willow was like a young girl dressing herself to go to a ball. Mara couldn't bear beauty that existed for itself alone. She decided to take home some of this beauty and put it in a vase. Let it serve some purpose. I assumed that she would break off one or two branches, say three at the most. The tree, of course, would be hurt, but it would bathe its wounds in sap and bind them up with bark to restore itself. To this day I can still see what Mara did. She didn't just break off a branch, but pulled it down towards her, tearing off a strip of the bark from the trunk. Then another, then a third and a fourth. She wrenched a whole layer from the unfortunate willow, flaying the tree alive as she stripped off the bark until the trunk was bare. We walked away. I turned around. The willow looked as if it had just emerged from Gestapo headquarters—lacerated, raped, battered into a vegetable equivalent of insensibility.

I should have turned away and left her, then and there, and to hell with the new flat and the extra room. But I knew that if I didn't see it through, nobody else would. In other words, I had to keep quiet and be tolerant. So I only asked, 'Why did you do that to the tree?'

'I act the way other people treat me,' Mara replied.

We walked on. Through my back I could feel the willow tree watching me go and thinking: 'How could you . . . ' And I thought of myself: 'How could you!'

A week passed. Bigboss returned. Not a word from Mara. I waited. I was not just waiting; I was living under the pressure of high-tension expectation. It was exhausting me; every nerve twanged like a taut wire. The only thing that could save me was to know something definite. I called up Mara. Feeling as if I were parachuting into a black abyss, I asked her, 'Has he come back?'

'Yes, he has,' said Mara calmly and with dignity.

'Have you spoken to him?'

'Yes, I have.'

She was silent, pretending not to know why I was calling her.

'Well? What was the result?' I could restrain myself no longer.

'Nothing,' said Mara, still calm and equally dignified. 'He said, "You bore me with your endless requests for favours. First I have to fund a hospital bed for your Tartar friend, Usmanov, then I must fix up this idiotic Artamonova woman with a new flat. Leave me alone.

Let me die in peace." The fact is, of course, he's not made of rubber,' Mara ended confidingly.

I had no idea who this Tartar Usmanov was; the 'idiotic Artamonova woman' was myself. I slammed down the receiver and went mad for the whole afternoon. My husband rejoiced. I had been taught a lesson. If I didn't respect someone, I shouldn't ask them for favours. By asking, I had lowered my moral standards. It was my own fault. It was natural justice: life is logical.

I had learned my lesson and drew some far-reaching conclusions from it, of which the chief one was: have nothing more to do with Mara. Ever. For whatever reason. When she called me, I immediately put down the receiver. The phone rang again and I didn't pick it up. In a sense, I was being a coward. I knew that if I answered it, I would say 'Yes', she would grab me by that 'yes' and haul me out of my lair; she would give off those hypnotic waves, suck me in with her electro-magnet and once again, like a rabbit, I would crawl into her maw.

Let her live her own life, and I would live mine. The poet Voznesensky once wrote: 'Survival is not enough for us: we have learned to cram more into life by squeezing the speedometers to go faster.' So I wouldn't be doing any more squeezing. My motto would be: slow and steady goes farthest. The only question is: farthest from *what*?

Five years passed.

Nothing happened in our country. Frightened by the Prague Spring, Brezhnev tried to make sure that nothing changed, that everything stayed as it was. No fresh streams should be allowed to flow. Life gradually turned into a swamp and was covered with duckweed.

Nothing happened in my personal life either. We went on living in our one-room flat, although in our co-operative block of flats there was constant movement: somebody died; somebody got divorced; somebody sailed away to other shores. Flats became available, but not for us. One had to bribe the chairman of the co-operative, but we didn't know how much to give him or how to do it. We were afraid of offending him.

I saw nothing of Mara, but echoes of her life reached me.

She was working in some prestigious institution attached to the Academy of Sciences. This was her new stamping-ground, in which she did whatever she wanted: sacking people, appointing them to jobs; promoting or holding up dissertations. It was a scene of continuous battle, with horses and riders tangled in heaps.

Mara had to be removed—but first of all neutralized. This fearsome task was taken on by a Professor Kartseva, a woman in charge of one of the laboratories. Kartseva was certain that Comrade Bigboss knew nothing of Mara's doings. His name was being blatantly used and thereby made vulnerable. Kartseva spoke to Bigboss on the closed internal telephone line, introduced herself, opened his eyes for him and replaced the receiver conscious that justice had been restored.

From then on the plot developed like a fairy story with an unhappy ending. Within a week, Kartseva's laboratory no longer existed. And since the laboratory was abolished, so was her job with its salary of 360 roubles a month. Her red Academy pass automatically became invalid, and the security guard on the gate no longer admitted her to the grounds. Mara roared with laughter, flashing her handsome white teeth.

And what became of Professor Kartseva, member of the Communist Party? Did she fight, or did she capitulate, aware that the struggle was hopeless? Nobody knows. People say she got a job as janitor in a block of flats, in order to have nothing more to do with the state machine. In winter you clear away the snow; in autumn you sweep up the leaves.

The victim had removed herself. The laboratory staff kept their mouths shut and took refuge in their offices like foxes going to ground. Toadies and time-servers sprouted like cornflowers in a field of grain. Mara savoured the taste of great and total power.

Dima, meanwhile, had met another woman, had started an affair with her and, like an honourable man, decided to marry her. When Mara heard of this, she made a couple of phone calls and Dima was put into a lunatic asylum. There he was stuffed full of drugs which made him fat and stupid and lacking in desire.

On his discharge, some friends gave him a Siamese cat. He called it Mara. After a while Mara gave birth to a kitten, named Kuzya. There being no one with whom he could leave the cats, when he went away on medical business or on holiday, he would pack the cats into a basket and take them with him.

Mara did not want to give him away to another woman. She had had enough of giving men away. Dima did not rebel. Like Kartseva, he submitted.

But there exists a balance in nature. If there is a hard winter, it means a hot summer. And vice versa. Retribution came to Mara from an unexpected direction—in the form of a junior research fellow, a student from the provinces by the name of Lomeyeva, who was unable to obtain a Moscow residence permit and so obliged to live beyond the city limits (hence the name given to this underprivileged caste: *limitchiks*).

Limitchiks are not like the soldiers of Napoleon's army who came and went away again. They are formidable shock troops, perpetually trying to storm the city's gates.

Lomeyeva came from the Urals. Her talents being small, she had to rely on her bottom rather than her head. A solid bottom can sit out as many as three dissertations. She also relied on her mouth: stored up behind each cheek was a withering charge of ball-lightning. When she spat them out, she could reduce an adversary to ashes. She had no need of other people's jobs or perks but she would never give up anything that she saw as hers. The data of her biography: born 1951; great-grandfather and grandfather died of vodka, the one at home, the other in a ditch. Her father was keeping up the glorious family tradition. Husband: army officer. Son: member of the Pioneers. Lomeyeva herself was a Party member, morally sound, ambitious and purposeful.

Where Mara had stars in her eyes and a fathomless abyss of ambition, Lomeyeva had greyness and dogged persistence. In the seventies, greyness and persistence were suitable attributes for a scientific career. The Brezhnev era was their time; their star was in the ascendant.

Mara, made careless by her apparent omnipotence, committed a fatal error. She unceremoniously laughed Lomeyeva's dissertation out of court, splattering it over the walls so thoroughly that you couldn't have scraped it off with a spoon. The dissertation failed to satisfy the examiners. Lomeyeva, in turn, lashed out with an incandescent blast of dragon's breath and unleashed a good dozen shots of her ball-lightning. Mara's dissertation was also held up in the final committee.

Horrified, everyone ran for cover, leaving the arena free for a battle royal. Mara and Lomeyeva were locked in combat.

Brezhnev died and was buried in Red Square. The hefty lads detailed to lower the coffin into the grave made a blunder in what should have been a co-ordinated movement, and the coffin dropped down with an awkward crash that reverberated all over the country. That bump was the start of a new era.

Andropov began to arouse people's hopes, but that beginning coincided with the end of his life. At the funeral, Chernenko was seen warming his hands on his ears. Or he may have been warming his ears with his hands. Nobody quite understood why he, ailing and chronically short of breath, looking like the personnel officer in some local Party committee, should have been pushed into such a demanding and responsible post. A year later he, too, was buried under the same Kremlin wall, and this time the television cameramen tactfully averted their lenses from the grave in case there should be another resounding bump. But the wheel of history cannot be turned back. A new Thaw had begun.

Comrade Bigboss was pensioned off. The seedy underside of the system began to be exposed. Lomeyeva pinned Mara to the ground. The stars in the heavens lined up in a configuration unpropitious to Mara. Her magnetic storm could no longer devastate all around it and, finding no outlet, turned inward on to Mara herself. Cancer flared up within her like a blow-torch. A malignant tumour, triggered by stress, exploded within her body. Perhaps, too, the fact that she had so often sunbathed without a bra was a contributory cause.

Mara was taken to hospital. Two surgeons worked on her, one standing by her breasts, the other by her crotch, and with their four hands they cut the woman out of Mara.

After the operation the rest of her humanity was attacked. She was subjected to chemotherapy and radiotherapy. She grew weak. Her hair fell out. But Mara survived. Hatred and the thirst for revenge proved to be stronger than cancer. Mara was like a

Pershing missile recalled for repairs while in full flight towards its target.

After a month she was discharged from hospital—half-alive, like the ravaged willow tree. She put on a wig and plunged into battle.

Some friends of hers brought her a pair of false breasts from France. The French make a cult of woman and they have the gift of anticipating a woman's needs in any situation. The prosthesis, made of soft plastic and filled with glycerine, looked extremely elegant. The complete imitation of a living body.

Mara wrapped this sad object in a lawn handkerchief and picked up Soms, whom she had inherited from her mother. Soms, a pug, was already old but looked like a puppy, as do all small dogs. Recently Mara had been avoiding people and her only company was the noble, loving Soms. And so—with the lawn-wrapped bundle in her hand and Soms on her shoulder—Mara went into the familiar office. But though the office was the old one, the Comrade Bigboss was a new one. And Mara was not her old self. She had no breasts to display now; in their place were scars, one running into the other, as though the cancer had clenched its jaw.

Mara untied the little bundle in front of Bigboss and said, 'This is what my colleagues have done to me.'

Somewhat naturally, Bigboss failed to understand her and asked, 'What is this?'

Mara briefly told him her story: the conflict with Lomeyeva; the stress-derived cancerous tumour; the resulting loss of her health and perhaps of her life. Mara had sacrificed her life in the fight for justice.

The new Comrade Bigboss, like the old one, was also human. He looked at Mara with horror, at her quivering little dog, at the glycerine breast lying in front of him on his own desk. He was struck by the transience of all living things. But after the thought about transience there came the wish that Mara should pick up her bodily parts, go away and not come back again.

But a person only goes away without coming back again when, as official terminology puts it, their case is decided.

Mara's case was decided. In the course of one month her dissertation passed all levels of scrutiny. At the final board, she defended her thesis brilliantly. She faced the examiners looking as shapely and elegant as a mannequin, with bright, skilfully rouged cheeks, artificial hair and artificial breasts. Artificial diamonds, like twin candelabra, dangled from her ears. But the gleam in her eyes was real. It never occurred to anyone present to see this triumphant, talented woman as a victim.

After the award of her degree, Mara phoned me at home. I went to the telephone without suspecting that it was her. Clearly her electro-magnetic powers had weakened and had ceased to operate at a distance.

'Congratulate me—I'm a master!'

I already knew about her illness. I knew the price she had paid for that dissertation. Why, after all, had she wanted a master's so much? Forty-five is the age for doctorates, not for master's degrees. Obviously Mara was possessed of a complex: having never given birth, having failed to bequeath her flesh, her legacy would be the thought contained in her dissertation. She wanted to leave behind a part of *herself*.

I sighed heavily. I said, 'Congratulations.'

Mara sensed the effort that my congratulations had cost me and put down the receiver. No doubt I had annoyed her.

Having won a victory, Mara lost her sense of purpose and came to a stop. The cancer thereupon raised its head again, crawled through her bones and along her spine. She found it harder and harder to start each day. Mara lay in the empty flat and imagined the doorbell ringing.

But no one rang the doorbell.

Mara would get up. Take a taxi. Drive to work. She now had her own office, with a plate on the door inscribed: 'M.P. Alexandrova, M. Ed.' Next door was Lomeyeva's office, adorned with a similar plate. Their battle had ended in a draw. Lomeyeva had not ceded an inch of her territory. So what if she would never scale the heights? Are the learned professions peopled exclusively by geniuses? Let us take, say, ginseng cream, which is sold in perfumery shops. How much ginseng is in it? One ten-thousandth of one per cent. The rest is vaseline. It's the same in the sciences. One genius—the rest vaseline. They, the rest, are the footsoldiers. Why shouldn't Lomeyeva be allowed to join the ranks? She was no worse than all the others.

Lomeyeva would walk past Mara's office, heels clacking on the floor—young, physically whole, with two breasts, size 38-C. She clattered past loudly, on purpose, the tap of each heel reverberating in Mara's head, as if nails were being driven into her brain. Mara would stuff a handkerchief into her mouth to stop herself groaning with pain.

In that period of her life I tried to keep in touch with her by telephone. But Mara resented my calls.

'Why do you keep ringing me?' she would ask. 'You think I don't know why you call me? You want to know whether I'm dead or not. Well, I'm alive—fancy that! I'm working. And I'm in love. I look fine. I'm going to start a new fashion: one breast. Like the Amazons. But you're so limited; you wouldn't have heard about the Amazons.'

I said nothing. I really know very little about the Amazons, except that they galloped about on horseback, used bows and arrows and, for convenience, cut off one breast.

'And do you know another reason why you call me?' Mara went on. 'You're frightened of cancer. And you want to know what it's like. What *it* is like for others. Isn't that so? Why don't you say something?'

I don't like it when people think I am worse than I am. Everyone has their ideal conception of their own self. And it upsets me when people devalue my ideal. But Mara was in a worse state than I was, and if she wanted to walk all over me, then I would let her.

'All right,' I said. 'From your voice, you sound pretty good to me.'

Mara paused. Then she said calmly, 'I'm dying, Larisa.'

Mara left no gravestone. She suspected that no one would ever visit it, and decided to have the last word herself: I don't *want* you to come. I have decided this, not you.

In her will, Mara instructed Dima to scatter her ashes over Leningrad. Dima didn't know how one did this. My husband explained that it would be best done from a helicopter. But how was one to get hold of a helicopter?

Dima took away the urn, which looked like a football trophy. Then one fine day he tipped the ashes into a polythene bag, took a ticket on a river-bus and set sail down the Neva.

It was a warm, balmy autumn day. The sun was working with its youthful, summer enthusiasm. A gentle breeze blew the hair back from his forehead. And the ashes, it seemed to Dima, flew away gently and gratefully.

Dima scattered Mara, her love, her talent and her electromagnetic storms. And the people standing on deck thought he was salting, or rather peppering, the water.

'A'.

A clean page. I write: 'Alexandrova, Mara Petrovna.' And I draw a black frame around the name. She has no memorial. Let it be here. In my address book. Among the living.

Sometimes I dream about her and then I think about her all the next day; I hold mental conversations with her and I have the strange feeling there's a discussion that we haven't finished and must continue. And I have another feeling, too: guilt. I feel guilty towards her. What for? I don't know. Or maybe I do know.

I go on with my life, but all the time I am continually turning round to look back and I seem to be going on my way with a permanent crick in my neck.

Translated from the Russian by Michael Glenny.

GRANTA BOOKS

Ryszard Kapuściński
The Soccer War

In 1964, Ryszard Kapuściński was appointed by the Polish Press
Agency as one of its only foreign correspondents, and for the next ten
years he was 'responsible' for fifty countries.
Kapuściński was the only correspondent in Honduras when, after a
World Cup qualifying match with El Salvador, the 'Soccer War' was
declared. Posted to Africa, he arrived in Zanzibar as revolution broke
out; fleeing to what was then called Tanganyika, he encountered a
coup. In Burundi he was sentenced to death by a firing-squad.
Kapuściński befriended Che Guevara in Bolivia, Allende in Chile and
Lumumba in the Congo. By the time he returned to Poland in 1980, he
had witnessed twenty-seven revolutions and coups.
The Soccer War is Kapuściński's story.

Hardback £12.99 ISBN 014014209-6
October 1990 publication

Lapidarium

Kapuściński's *Lapidarium* is a journal of the last twenty years. Ranging
from London to Gdansk, Mexico City to Warsaw, the Yucatan to Palo
Alto, it is more than a simple account of Poland. It is also
Kapuściński's account of Poland *and* the rest of the world, of those
moments poised between two cultures, the east and the west, in the
years before the revolution of 1989.

A paperback original £4.99 ISBN 0140 14026-3
October 1990 publication

HANS MAGNUS
ENZENSBERGER
EUROPE IN RUINS

German troops surrendering, 1944.

A few days before I left Luanda, I was taken by American friends to dine in a black-market restaurant. We ate at outside tables in a little enclosure on the street. The clientele all looked more or less as if they were black-market profiteers themselves. We were sitting right next to the rail that fenced us in from the street, and I had my back to this, so that, absorbed in conversations, I did not notice at first that a crowd had gathered behind us and were reaching in to grab things from our plates. But the management soon sent out a bouncer, who knocked down an old woman with a blow on the head and drove back the mob, mostly women and children, some of whom disappeared, while others, keeping their distance, stood dumbly and stared at the diners.

Here in Beirut refugees are lying on all the steps, and one has the impression that they would not look up even were a miracle to take place in the middle of the square; so certain are they that none will happen. One could tell them that some country beyond the Lebanon was prepared to accept them and they would gather up their boxes, without really believing. Their life is unreal, a waiting without expectation, and they no longer cling to it: rather, life clings to them, ghostlike, an unseen beast which grows hungry and drags them through ruined railway stations, day and night, in sunshine and in rain; it breathes in the sleeping children as they lie on the rubble, their heads between bony arms, curled up like embryos in the womb, as if longing to return there.

Unsettling about this place in the North of Sri Lanka is not that one fears being molested—at any rate not during the day—but, rather, because of the sure knowledge that people of one's own sort, if suddenly faced with living this kind of life, would go under within three days. One feels very keenly that even a life like this has its own laws, and it would take years to learn them. A truck full of policemen; at once they scatter, some stand still and grin, while I look on and have no idea what is happening. Four boys and three girls are loaded into the truck, where they squat down among others who have already been picked up elsewhere. Indifferent, impenetrable. The police have helmets and automatics, therefore authority, but no knowledge. The newspapers carry a daily column of street attacks, sometimes naked corpses are discovered, and the murderers come as a rule from the other side. Whole districts without a single light. A landscape of brick hills, beneath them the buried, above them twinkling stars; nothing stirs there but rats.

Reports from the Third World, such as we can read every morning over breakfast. The place names are false, however. The locations are not, in fact, Luanda, Beirut and Trincomalee; they are Rome, Frankfurt-am-Main and Berlin. Only forty-five years separate us from conditions we have become accustomed to thinking of as African, Asian or Latin American.

At the end of the Second World War Europe was a pile of ruins, not merely in a physical sense; it seemed totally bankrupt in political and moral terms. It was not only the defeated Germans for whom the situation seemed hopeless. When Edmund Wilson came to London in July 1945, he found the English in a state of collective depression. The mood of the city reminded him of the cheerlessness of Moscow: 'How empty, how sickish, how senseless everything suddenly seems the moment the war is over! We are left flat with the impoverished and humiliating life that the drive against the enemy kept our minds off. Where our efforts have all gone toward destruction, we have been able to build nothing at home to fall back on amidst our own ruin.'

No one dared believe that the devastated continent could have a future. It seemed as if the history of Europe had come to an end with an overwhelming act of self-destruction, which the Germans had initiated and completed with savage energy: 'This is what exists,' noted Max Frisch in the spring of 1946, 'the grass growing in the houses, the dandelions in the churches and suddenly one can imagine, how it might all continue to grow, how a forest might creep over our cities, slowly, inexorably, thriving unaided by human hands, a silence of thistles and moss, an earth without history, only the twittering of birds, spring, summer and autumn, the breathing of years which there is no one to count any more.'

If someone had prophesied to the cave-dwellers of Dresden or Warsaw of those days a future like that of 1990, they would have thought him crazy. But for people today their own past has become just as unimaginable. They have long repressed and forgotten it and those who are younger lack the imagination and the knowledge to make a picture of earlier times. It grows increasingly difficult to imagine the condition of our continent at the end of the Second World War. The story-tellers, apart from Böll, Primo Levi, Hans Werner Richter, Louis-Ferdinand Céline and Curzio Malaparte and a few others, capitulated before the subject; the so-called *Trümmerliteratur*—literature of the ruins— hardly delivered what it promised.

Period newsreels show monotonous pictures of destruction; the soundtrack consists of hollow phrases; the films provide no indication of the inner state of men and women in the devastated cities. The memoir literature that emerged later lacks authority. This is not only because of the urge to touch things up which is so frequent in the genre of autobiography, or because the authors usually tend towards self-justification and self-accusation. It is not their integrity that is questionable, but their perspective. In looking back, they lose the very thing which should matter most: the coincidence of the observer with what he is looking at. The best sources tend to be the eyewitness accounts of contemporaries.

Anyone studying the eyewitness reports will, however, have an odd experience. A key feature of the post-war period is a strange ignorance, a narrowing of horizons, that is unavoidable under extreme living conditions. At best it is a straightforward lack of knowledge of the world, easily explained by the years of isolation. John Gunther writes of a young soldier in Warsaw, with whom he entered into conversation on a summer evening in

Berlin, 1945.

1948: 'There was no nonsense about him. He knew exactly what Poland had suffered and what he himself had suffered. His ignorance of the outside world was, however, considerable. He had never met an American before. He wanted to know if New York had been made *kaputt* by the war like Warsaw.'

Americans were looked at as if they were men from Mars, and their belongings were treated with a reverence reminiscent of the cargo cults of Polynesia. Europeans displayed attitudes like those found in the Third World. Someone who is thinking only of the next meal, who is forced to build a roof over his own head, will lack the desire and energy to make himself aware and well-informed. The restricted vision was compounded by the absence of freedom of movement. Millions were on the move, but only to save their skins. Travel in the usual sense of the word was not possible.

In the first years after the war the long-term consequences of the Fascist dictatorship were becoming evident, not only in Germany but throughout Europe. Europeans took shelter behind a collective amnesia. Reality was not just ignored; it was flatly denied. With a mixture of lethargy, defiance and self-pity they regressed to a kind of second childhood. Anyone meeting this syndrome for the first time was astonished; it seemed to be a form of *moral insanity*. When she visited the Rhineland in April 1945, the American journalist Martha Gellhorn was exasperated, indeed staggered, by the statements of the Germans she met:

> No one is a Nazi. No one ever was. There may have been some Nazis in the next village, and as a matter of fact, that town about twenty kilometres away was a veritable hotbed of Nazidom. To tell you the truth, confidentially, there were a lot of Communists here. We were always known as very Red. Oh, the Jews? Well, there weren't really many Jews in this neighbourhood. Two, maybe six. They were taken away. I hid a Jew for six weeks. I hid a Jew for eight weeks. (I hid a Jew, he hid a Jew, all God's chillun hid Jews.) We have nothing against the Jews; we always got on well with them. We have had enough of this government. Ah, how we have

suffered. The bombs. We lived in the cellars for weeks. We welcome the Americans. We do not fear them; we have no reason to fear. We have done nothing wrong; we are not Nazis.

It should, we feel, be set to music. Then the Germans could sing this refrain and that would make it even better. They all talk like this. One asks oneself how the detested Nazi government, to which no one paid allegiance, managed to carry on this way for five and a half years. Obviously not a man, woman or child in Germany ever approved of the war for a minute, according to them. We stand around looking blank and contemptuous and listen to this story without friendliness and certainly without respect. To see a whole nation passing the buck is not an enlightening spectacle.

More than two years later Janet Flanner comes to similar conclusions:

The new Germany is bitter against everyone else on earth, and curiously self-satisfied. Bursting with complaints of her hunger, lost homes, and other sufferings, she considers without interest or compassion the pains and losses she imposed on others, and she expects and takes, usually with carping rather than thanks, charity from those nations she tried to destroy . . . The significant Berlin catch-all phrase is 'That was the war, but this is the peace.' This cryptic remark means, in free translation, that the people feel no responsibility for the war, which they regard as an act of history, and that they consider the troubles and confusions of the peace the Allies' fault. People here never mention Hitler's name any more. They just say darkly *Früher war es besser,'* (Things were better before), meaning under Hitler. Only a few Germans seem to remember that, beginning with the occupations of 1940, some of them had the sense to launch the slogan 'Enjoy the war. The peace will be terrible.' It is.

So much for the state of consciousness of the Germans. Other Europeans were no less deluded. John Gunther reports: 'I asked one responsible Greek politician what the solution was, if any, and he replied in one word, "War." Indeed many conservative Greeks feel that nothing but outright war between the United States and the Soviet Union can rescue them; they actively want a war, horrible as this may seem, and make no bones about it. I asked my friend, "But do you think there is going to be a war?" He answered, "Europe is in anarchy. One hundred million people are slaves. We *have* to have war. There *must* be a war, or we will lose everything."'

Anyone who turns to published opinion of the time in the hope of gaining a clearer picture of post-war Europe faces further disappointments. Sober verdicts, intelligent analyses, convincing reportage are hardly to be found in the newspaper and magazine columns of the years 1945–48. That is not solely due to restrictions imposed by the occupying powers. The internal self-censorship of journalists was of much greater consequence. The Germans distinguished themselves in this respect too. Most intellectuals failed to bear witness to the facts and fled into abstraction. One searches in vain for the great reportage. What one finds, along with philosophical generalizations on the theme of collective guilt, are invocations of the Western tradition, of Goethe, humanism, the forgetfulness of being and the 'idea of freedom'. These exercises seem to indicate a near total loss of reality.

For all of these reasons little reliance can be placed on the testimony of participants in the events in Europe. One must go to other sources to gain an accurate picture of post-war conditions. The most trustworthy source is the gaze of the *outsider*. The most acute reports were provided by authors who accompanied the victorious Allied armies. The finest among them are the American reporters, journalists like Janet Flanner and Martha Gellhorn and writers like Edmund Wilson, who did not feel superior to the press. They were part of the great Anglo-Saxon tradition of literary reportage—the Europeans have, until now, failed to produce anything to equal it. Other valuable sources

Aachen, 1945.

Photo: Hulton-Deutsch Collection

were the product of chance, like the confidential reports of an American editor who worked for the US secret service, or the notes of *émigrés* who attempted to return to the Old World. Authors from countries which the war had spared, like the Swiss Max Frisch and the Swedish novelist Stig Dagerman, also made contributions.

All of these witnesses came from a world which was similar to ours: orderly, normal, characterized by the thousand things taken for granted in a functioning civil society. The sense of shock that the European disaster produced in them was all the greater for the contrast with their experience at home. They could hardly trust their eyes before the brutal, eccentric, terrifying and moving scenes which they experienced in Paris and Naples, in the villages of Crete and the catacombs of Warsaw. The stranger's gaze is able to make us comprehend what was happening in Europe then; it does not rely on the linguistic rules of ideology, but on the telling physical detail. While the leading articles and policy statements of the period have a strange mustiness about them, the eyewitness reports remain fresh.

The specialists in perception are at their best when they generalize least, when they do not censor the fantastic contradictions of the chaotic world through which they are moving, but leave them as they are. Max Frisch concludes his notes on Berlin with a laconic remark that silences all critical argument: 'A landscape of brick hills, beneath them the buried, above them the twinkling stars; nothing stirs there but rats. —Evening at the theatre: Iphigenia.'

A good example of the astonishing foresight that emerges in the texts of the outsiders is Martha Gellhorn's reportage of July 1944. It was a time when not a soul in Washington was thinking about the Cold War. In the middle of an artillery duel in a village on the Adriatic, Martha Gellhorn converses with soldiers of a Polish unit fighting against the Germans:

> They had come a long way from Poland. They call themselves the Carpathian Lancers because most of them escaped from Poland over the Carpathian mountains. They had been gone from their country for

Essen, 1946.

Photo: Popperfoto

almost five years. For three and a half years this cavalry regiment, which was formed in Syria, fought in the Middle East and the Western Desert. Last January they returned to their own continent of Europe, via Italy, and it was the Polish Corps, with this armoured regiment fighting in it as infantry, that finally took Cassino in May. In June they started their great drive up the Adriatic, and the prize, Ancona—which this regiment had entered first—lay behind us.

It is a long road home to Poland, to the great Carpathian mountains, and every mile of road has been bought most bravely. But now they do not know what they are going home to. They fight an enemy in front of them and fight him superbly. And with their whole hearts they fear an ally, who is already in their homeland. For they do not believe that Russia will relinquish their country after the war; they fear that they are to be sacrificed in this peace, as Czechoslovakia was in 1938. It must be remembered that almost every one of these men, irrespective of rank, class or economic condition, has spent time in either a German or a Russian prison during this war. It must be remembered that for five years they have had no news from their families, many of whom are still prisoners in Russia or Germany. It must be remembered that these Poles have only twenty-one years of national freedom behind them, and a long aching memory of foreign rule.

So we talked of Russia and I tried to tell them that their fears must be wrong or there would be no peace in the world. That Russia must be as great in peace as she has been in war, and that the world must honour the valour and suffering of the Poles by giving them freedom to rebuild and better their homeland. I tried to say I could not believe that this war which is fought to maintain the rights of man will end by ignoring the rights of Poles. But I am not a Pole; I belong to a large free country and I speak with the optimism of those who are forever safe. And I remember the tall gentle twenty-

Berlin, 1947.

two-year-old soldier who drove me in a jeep one day, and how quietly he explained that his father had died of hunger in a German prison camp, and his mother and sister had been silent for four years in a labour camp in Russia, and his brother was missing, and he had no profession because he had entered the army when he was seventeen and so had had no time to learn anything. Remembering this boy, and all the others I knew, with their appalling stories of hardship and homelessness, it seemed to me that no American had the right to talk to the Poles, since we had never even brushed such suffering ourselves.

The editors of *Collier's* magazine, for which Martha Gellhorn was working, refused to publish this report, because the Poles' prophetic remarks about the Soviet Union, the United States' most important ally, did not suit them.

What makes the work of these reporters so illuminating is not that they lay claim to a higher objectivity, but the reverse, that they hold on to their radically subjective viewpoint. This is true even when—yes, especially when—they put themselves in the wrong. Among the costs of immediacy is that one is infected by one's surroundings and cannot stand above them. The sore points from the post-war years emerge all the more clearly; the frictions between English and Americans, the fury of the victors at the grandiose impudence of the Neapolitans, above all the hatred of the Germans, which in some observers mounts to disgust and a desire for revenge. Whoever had behaved like the Germans and continued to behave like them—that is, outside all reason—could not expect any *fairness*; almost all representatives of the victorious nations were convinced of that, and it is by no means superfluous to remind oneself of the extreme expressions of feeling during those years.

The observers from neutral countries are more ambivalent in their judgements. Not that one could accuse them of special sympathy for the Germans; but they are more able than the victors to perceive their own role. After a visit to Germany in the autumn of 1946, the Swede Stig Dagerman writes:

Frankfurt, 1947.

Don't miss out on major issues.

Every issue of Granta features politics, polemic, travel writing, fiction and more. So don't miss out – subscribe today and save up to 31%.

Name _____

Address _____

_____

_____ Postcode _____

B1331

Please enter my subscription for: ☐ Four issues £19.95

☐ Eight issues £37 ☐ Twelve issues £49.95

Please start my subscription with issue number _____

Payment: ☐ Cheque enclosed

☐ Access/American Express/Visa/Diners Club

Expiry date _____

☐☐☐☐☐☐☐☐☐☐☐☐☐☐☐

Signature _____

Overseas postage: Europe: Please add £6 per year. Outside Europe: £12 per year air-speeded, £20 per year airmail.

Please tick this box if you do not want to receive direct mail from other companies ☐

UP TO 31% OFF

Don't miss out on major issues.

Every issue of Granta features politics, polemic, travel writing, fiction and more. So don't miss out – subscribe today and save up to 31%.

Name _____

Address _____

_____

_____ Postcode _____

B1332

Please enter my subscription for: ☐ Four issues £19.95

☐ Eight issues £37 ☐ Twelve issues £49.95

Please start my subscription with issue number _____

Payment: ☐ Cheque enclosed

☐ Access/American Express/Visa/Diners Club

Expiry date _____

☐☐☐☐☐☐☐☐☐☐☐☐☐☐☐

Signature _____

Overseas postage: Europe: Please add £6 per year. Outside Europe: £12 per year air-speeded, £20 per year airmail.

Please tick this box if you do not want to receive direct mail from other companies ☐

UP TO 31% OFF

NO
STAMP
REQUIRED

Granta
FREEPOST
2-3, Hanover Yard
Noel Road
London
N1 8BR

NO
STAMP
REQUIRED

Granta
FREEPOST
2-3, Hanover Yard
Noel Road
London
N1 8BR

If any commentary is to be risked on the mood of bitterness towards the Allies, mixed with self-contempt, with apathy, with comparisons to the disadvantage of the present—all of which were certain to strike the visitor that gloomy autumn—it is necessary to keep in mind a whole series of particular occurrences and physical conditions. It is important to remember that statements implying dissatisfaction with or even distrust of the goodwill of the victorious democracies were made not in an airless room or on a theatrical stage echoing with ideological repartee but in all too palpable cellars in Essen, Hamburg or Frankfurt-am-Main. Our autumn picture of the family in the waterlogged cellar also contains a journalist who, carefully balancing on planks set across the water, interviews the family on their views of the newly constituted democracy in their country, asks them about their hopes and illusions, and, above all, asks if the family was better off under Hitler. The answer that the visitor then receives has this result: stooping with rage, nausea and contempt, the journalist scrambles hastily backwards out of the stinking room, jumps into his hired English car or American jeep, and half an hour later over a drink or a good glass of real German beer, in the bar of the press hotel composes a report on the subject 'Nazism is alive in Germany'.

Fifty years after the catastrophe Europe understands itself more than ever as a common project, yet it is far from achieving a comprehensive analysis of the years immediately following the Second World War. The memory of the period is incomplete and provincial, if it is not entirely lost in repression or nostalgia. People were busy with their own survival and could not bother with larger events; now they are reluctant to talk about skeletons in the cupboard. They prefer to address the glowing future of the Common Market or the opening up of Eastern Europe, instead of thinking about the unpleasant times when no one would have put a brass farthing on a rebirth of our peninsula. This is a fatal strategy; in retrospect it appears that during the years 1944–48, without the participants suspecting it, the seeds were sown not only of future successes but also of future conflicts.

A high-explosive bomb is a high-explosive bomb, a desperate hunger does not distinguish between black and white, just and unjust, but neither the destructive power of the air forces nor the post-war misery was capable of homogenizing Europe and extinguishing its differences. What was not visible in the burnt earth proved to be of considerable consequence: the tenacious ability to survive of the immaterial structures which had, as it were, hibernated in people's heads. The European societies were like cities which had been destroyed, but for which detailed construction diagrams and land registers had been preserved; their invisible connections and network plans had survived the destruction. Differences in traditions, capacities, mentalities endured and re-emerged.

As Norman Lewis wrote in his Naples reportage of 1944:

It is astonishing to witness the struggles of this city so shattered, so starved, so deprived of all those things that justify a city's existence, to adapt itself to a collapse into conditions which must resemble life in the Dark Ages. People camp out like Bedouins in deserts of brick. There is little food, little water, no salt, no soap. A lot of Neapolitans have lost their possessions, including most of their clothing, in the bombings, and I have seen some strange combinations of garments about the streets, including a man in an old dinner-jacket, knickerbockers and army boots, and several women in lacy confections that might have been made up from curtains. There are no cars but carts by the hundred, and a few antique coaches such as barouches and phaetons drawn by lean horses. Today at Posilippo I stopped to watch the methodical dismemberment of a stranded German half-track by a number of youths who were streaming away from it like leaf-cutter ants, carrying pieces of metal of all shapes and sizes. Fifty yards away a well-dressed lady with a feather in her hat squatted to milk a goat.

At the water's edge below, two fishermen had roped together several doors salvaged from the ruins, piled their gear on these and were about to go fishing. Inexplicably no boats are allowed out, but nothing is said in the proclamation about rafts. Everyone improvises and adapts.

The attitudes that Lewis describes have remained characteristic of the population of southern Italy up to the present day: an ingenuity which knows how to take advantage of every opening, a parasitism of quite heroic energy and an untiring readiness to exploit a hostile world. The priorities of the French were, and still are, quite different. In February 1945 Janet Flanner writes:

The brightest news here is the infinite resilience of the French as human beings. Parisians are politer and more patient in their troubles than they were in their prosperity. Though they have no soap that lathers, both men and women smell civilized when you encounter them in the Métro, which everybody rides in, there being no buses or taxis. Everything here is a substitute for something else. The women who are not neat, thin, and frayed look neat, thin, and chic clattering along in their platform shoes of wood—substitute for shoe leather— which sound like horses' hoofs. Their broad-shouldered, slightly shabby coats of sheepskin—substitute for wool cloth which the Nazis preferred for themselves—were bought on the black market three winters ago. The Paris midinettes, for whom, because of their changeless gaiety, there is really no substitute on earth . . . still wear their home-made, fantastically high, upholstered Charles X turbans. Men's trousers are shabby, since they are not something which can be run up at home. The young intellectuals of both sexes go about in ski clothes. This is what the resistance wore when it was fighting and freezing outdoors in the *maquis*, and it has set the Sorbonne undergraduate style.

The more serious normalities of traditional Paris life go

Berlin, 1949.

on, in readjusted form. Candy shops display invitations to come in and register for your sugar almonds, the conventional sweet for French baptisms, but you must have a doctor's certificate swearing that you and your wife are really expecting. Giddy young wedding parties that can afford the price pack off to the wedding luncheon two by two in *vélo-taxis*, bicycle-barouches which are hired for hundreds of francs an hour. The other evening your correspondent saw a more modest bridal couple starting off on their life journey together in the Métro. They stood apart from everyone else on the Odéon platform, the groom in his rented *smoking* and with a boutonnière, the bride all in white—that is, a white raincoat, white rubber boots, white sweater and skirt, white turban, and a large, old-fashioned white nosegay. They were holding hands. American soldiers across the tracks shouted good wishes to them.

Of course the descriptions express the prejudices and *idées reçues* of the observers. But they also rise above conventional thinking. The following reportage by John Gunther flies in the face of almost every cliché about the Poles.

This concentrated tornado of pure useless horror turned Warsaw into Pompeii. I heard a serious-minded Pole say, 'Perhaps a few cats may have been alive, but certainly not a dog.' After liberation early in 1945 the Polish government took the heroic decision to rebuild. This was a herculean step, and Poles nowadays laugh about it with a peculiar rough tenderness, saying that the reason must have been their 'romanticism'. Even ministers as powerful as Hilary Minc thought that it would be impossible to rebuild, and suggested starting from scratch with a new capital at Lodz. He was outvoted. The decision to rebuild Warsaw, and keep it the capital no matter at what cost, was of course wise—and not romantic at all—in that it gave the patriotic focus and an urgent aggressive faith to the workings of the new regime . . .

133

Every Pole I met was almost violent with hope. 'See that?' A cabinet minister pointed to something that looked like a smashed gully. 'In twenty years time that will be our Champs Elysées.'

Particularly impressive is [the work of rebuilding] in the Old City, which is almost as complete a ruin as the ghetto. A patch of ravaged brick is all that remains of the Angelski Hotel where Napoleon stayed. The old bricks are used in the new structures, which gives a crazy patchwork effect. Hundreds of houses are only half rebuilt; as soon as a single room is habitable, people move in. I never saw anything more striking than the way a few pieces of timber shore up a shattered heap of stone or brick, so that a kind of perchlike room or nest is made available to a family, high over crumbling ruins. One end of a small building may be a pile of dust; at the other end you will see curtains in the windows.

Much of this furious reconstruction is done by voluntary labour; most, moreover, is done by human hand. Even cabinet ministers go out and work on Sunday. In all Warsaw, there are not more than two or three concrete mixers and three or four electric hoists; in all Warsaw, not one bulldozer! A gang of men climb up a wall, fix an iron hook on the end of a rope to the topmost bricks, climb down and pull. Presto!—the wall crashes. Then some distorted bricks go into what is going up. The effect is almost like that of double exposure in a film. No time for correct masonry!

So this catastrophically gutted city, probably the most savage ruin ever made by the hand of evil mankind anywhere, is being transformed into a new metropolis boiling and churning with vigour. Brick by brick, minute by minute, hand by hand, Warsaw is being made to live again through the fixed creative energy and imagination of an immensely gifted and devoted people.

Another writer observed the beginnings of German reconstruction on a journey through southern Germany. The reflections which Alfred Döblin set to paper have lost none of their force over the past decades.

A principal impression made by the country, and it provokes the greatest astonishment in someone arriving at the end of 1945, is that the people are running back and forward in the ruins like ants whose nest has been destroyed. Agitated and eager to work, their major grievance is that they cannot set to immediately, because of the absence of materials, the absence of directives.

The destruction does not make them depressed, but acts as an intense stimulus to work. I am convinced: If they had the means that they lack, they would rejoice tomorrow, only rejoice, that their old, out-of-date, badly laid out towns have been destroyed and that now they have been given the opportunity to put down something first-class, altogether modern . . .

In Stuttgart people talk to me and show me certain groups of buildings and state: that was this air raid or that air raid and recount certain episodes. And that is all. No particular information follows, and there are certainly not any further reflections. People go to their work, stand in queues here, as everywhere else, for food.

Already there are theatres, concerts and cinemas here and there and I hear, all have large audiences. The trams are running, horribly full as everywhere. People are practical and help one another. They worry about today and tomorrow in a way that is already troubling the thoughtful.

The countryside looks cared for. Only the cities are devastated. And how devastated. Out in America one has seen pictures of these cities in the cinemas. One can walk along the streets of many cities, the roadway and often the pavement too has been cleared. Almost everywhere the usable bricks have already been sorted out and neatly piled against the walls of buildings. They await a new use. For as I already said, here lives as before an industrious, orderly people. They have, as always, obeyed a

East Germany, 1949.

government, finally that of Hitler, and by and large do not understand, why this time obedience is supposed to have been bad. It will be much easier to rebuild their cities than to make them experience, what they have experienced and to understand how it came about.

One may find it unjust that the verdict on the reconstruction efforts of the people of Stuttgart is so ill-humoured by comparison with the praise bestowed on the rebuilding of Warsaw. But one cannot understand the puzzling energy of the Germans if one resists the idea that they have turned their defects into virtues. They had, in a quite literal sense, lost their minds and that was the condition of their future success. The tricky quality of this relationship emerges in the following report by Robert Thompson Pell, an American secret service officer, who in the spring of 1945 was faced with examining the activities during the Third Reich of the top managers of the I.G. Farben company.

On the whole I gained the impression that the German leaders had gone over to accommodating themselves to necessity—that, however, only to a limited degree. In the meanwhile they are sounding out our weak points, putting us to the test at every opportunity, trying to find out if we really mean it when we thump the table, and offering as much resistance as they dare. They say almost openly, we will not be able to cope with the situation ourselves and will have to turn to them again in the end. They are relying on us making so many mistakes that it will be inevitable that they take charge again. Till then they will bide their time and look on, while we bungle everything. Apart from that they play up the 'red peril' as much as they dare. As soon as one shows oneself to be even a little approachable—or if they believe they can see signs of it—they tell us again and again: 'We are so glad that you are here and not the Russians,' and in a few cases they've actually maintained that the German army withdrew so that we could save as much of West Germany from the Russians as could be saved.

The directors whom I fetched in my jeep every day

were itching to tell me that the German people had been
the victim of a worldwide conspiracy which had
intended to deliver up this lovely country to unknown
forces; Germany had conducted a defensive war; the
Allied 'terror raids' had united the German people, had
no military value and had been a serious error; they
were the true defenders of Western civilization against
'the Asiatic hordes' etc.

In short, the country was in chaos and the people
were in a hysterical condition, which quickly grew into
an attitude of defiance and a feeling of being treated
unjustly, and which was not clouded by the least trace
of guilt. Most of these men of high and in some cases
the highest standing in society were ready to admit, that
Germany had lost the war, but were quick to add the
reason was the superiority of the Allies in power and
material; they then immediately added in future they
would try to make that good. The overall impression
was, in short, disquieting. So far as I could ascertain,
the attitude of the average manager was characterized
by self-pity, fawning self-justification and an injured
sense of innocence, which was accompanied by a
yammering for pity and for aid in the reconstruction of
his devastated country. Many of them, if not the
majority, confidently expect that American capital will
commit itself without delay to the work of
reconstruction, and they declared themselves ready to
place their labour power and their intellect at the service
of these temporary masters; as a consequence they
openly expect to rebuild a Germany more powerful and
bigger than it was in the past.

These delusions of 1945 have since become, in a rather
roundabout way, reality, and the implicit historical irony
has turned into a sneer. That those who were defeated, the
Germans and the Japanese, today feel like victors is more than a
moral scandal; it is a political provocation. Our leaders never tire
of protesting that in the meantime we have all become peaceable,
democratic and moderate; in a word, well-behaved. The most

remarkable thing about this assertion is that it is true. The form that this mutation has taken with the Germans is to have turned them into a nation of shopkeepers. In that they are by no means alone. All the nations of Europe are with varying success trying to do the same. The German suicide attempt has failed, as has that of Europe as a whole. But the more our peninsula moves back into the centre of world politics and of the world market, the more a new kind of Eurocentrism will gain ground. A slogan that was copyrighted by Joseph Goebbels has reappeared in public debate: 'Fortress Europe'. It was once meant in a military sense; it has returned as an economic and demographic concept. A Europe in renewal will do well to remind itself of Europe in ruins, from which it is separated by only a few decades.

Translated from the German by Martin Chalmers.

The Max Frisch quotations are from his *Sketchbook: 1946–1949*, translated by Geoffrey Skelton (Harcourt Brace Jovanovich 1977).

GRANTA BOOKS

John Berger
Once in Europa

'Stories remarkable for their visionary intimacy.'
Angela Carter, *New York Times Book Review*

'These stories, once read, will not easily be forgotten, they are that
compelling.'
Guardian

'Berger's novel reminds us of something that much contemporary
writing tempts us to forget: that the greatest writers are
distinguished, ultimately, by the quality of their humanity.'
Sunday Times

'The extraordinary effect of these stories—a very strong collection
indeed—lies in the refusal to judge or lament. The author is not
pretending to be a peasant, nor is he a deliberate outsider. His role is
more delicately poised, creating stories which might help his fellow
villager, as well as the rest of us, to see the historical forces
that are affecting them.'
New Statesman & Society

Hardback £10.95 ISBN 0140-14207-X

Once in Europa is the second novel of John Berger's trilogy *Into their Labours*.
The third part, *Lilac and Flag,* will be published by Granta Books in January
1990. Copies at £12.99 can be reserved now by writing to Granta Books, 2-3
Hanover Yard, Noel Road, London N1 8BE.

CHRISTA WOLF
WHAT REMAINS

Alarmed, as if a bell inside me were ringing a warning, I jumped up this morning and found myself barefoot on the beautiful patterned carpet in the back room, saw myself throwing open the curtains and the window to the overflowing dustbins and rubble in the courtyard, which was deserted, as if abandoned for ever by the children with their bicycles and radios, by the plumbers and builders, even by Mrs G who would come down later in her apron dress and her green knitted hat to take the boxes from the seed shop, the perfumery and the Intershop out of the big wire containers, press them flat, tie them up into handy bundles and then take the bundles to the junk dealer round the corner in her four-wheeled handcart. She would complain loudly about the tenants, who, out of laziness, threw their bottles into the dustbins, about the people who came home late and broke open the front door almost every night because they forgot their key again and again, about the municipal housing department which didn't manage to install an electric door bell, but most of all about the drunks from the hotel restaurant next door who brazenly pissed in the broken open doorway.

The little diversions I allow myself every morning: clear a couple of newspapers from the table and put them in the magazine rack, smooth out table-cloths in passing, collect glasses, hum a song, knowing that in fact, as if drawn along on a string, I was on my way to the front room, to the big bay window that looked on to Friedrichstrasse and through which no sunlight came, because there is not much sun this spring, but still morning light, which I love, and a decent supply of which I wanted to store up, to live on in dark times.

So I stood, as every morning, behind the curtains, which had been put up recently so that I could hide behind them, and looked, hopefully unseen, across to the big car-park on the other side of Friedrichstrasse.

They were not there.

If I saw properly, all the parked cars in the first and second rows of the car park were empty. Two years ago, I had been deceived by the high head-rests of some cars, had believed them to be heads and uneasily admired their immobility; not that I don't make mistakes now, but I am past that stage. Heads are irregular in shape and they move; head-rests are regular, rounded, smooth—a huge difference which some day I will describe exactly.

I'd only like to know why yesterday they stayed there until after midnight and this morning they have simply disappeared.

I brushed my teeth, combed my hair, used various sprays, dressed in yesterday's trousers and pullover as I was not expecting anyone and could be alone: the best hope of the day. Back to the window; again nothing. It was a relief, I said to myself; but did I mean to say instead that I was waiting for them? I had made a fool of myself yesterday evening; some day I would probably feel embarrassed to think that every half-hour I had groped my way forward to the window in the darkened room to peep through a gap in the curtains. But why were three young gentlemen sitting for hours on end in a white Wartburg directly opposite our window?

Question marks: in future please take the placing of signs more seriously, I said to myself. In general: stick more to harmless agreements. That used to work, before. When? When there were more exclamation marks than question marks after sentences? I put on water. White, why on earth white? Why not, as in previous weeks, tomato-red, steel-blue? As if the colours or the make of the car were significant. As if the shadowy logic by which one vehicle replaced another and occupied a different space in the car-park was evidence of any kind of secret pattern. As if it could be worth thinking about the occupants of those cars—two, three strong, able-bodied young men in plain clothes, who had no other occupation except to look over at my window—and what they might want.

The coffee has to be strong and hot, filtered; the egg not too soft; home-made preserves; black bread. Luxury! Luxury! I thought every morning when I saw it all together. I hardly heard the news on the Western radio station (energy crisis, executions in Iran, strategic arms limitation agreement: themes of the past!), but gazed at the iron bar jammed across the doorway which secures the second entrance to our flat—the door, which opens on to the back stairs that lead from the kitchen down to the courtyard—against break-ins. It occurred to me that in my night-time dream this unused, narrow, filthy stairway, full of discarded furniture had been clean and filled with people whom in my dream I called 'riff-raff'—a word which I would never ever allow these wiry, agile, lemur-like men, who lacked any sense of shame, to hear. These men who had (what I had always feared so much!) gained admittance to my kitchen by the completely secure back door, and crowded around the threshold, pressed against the iron bar, which held firmly and was strangely respected by those miserable people, who could so easily have slipped through, but instead squashed their bodies against it, while more and more different figures, all unbelievably agile and eloquent, spewed of out some gate of hell invisible to me. What had they actually said? That we should not let ourselves be put out. That we should behave as if they weren't there at all. That it would be best if we forgot them completely. They were not taunting us, they were serious, that was what embittered me most. But since one cannot prevent one's own dream I forced myself to laugh out loud.

D on't be afraid. My other language—I thought, still eager to deceive myself, as I put the dishes in the sink, made my bed, went back into the front room and at last sat at my desk—my other language would be bold (that much at least I believed I could anticipate), considerate and loving. It would hurt no one but myself. It began to dawn on me why I could not get further than these scraps of paper, further than writing isolated sentences and pretending to be reflecting on them: in reality I was thinking nothing.

They were there again.

It was five past nine. They had been there again for three minutes. I had noticed immediately. I had felt a jolt like the motion inside me of a clock hand that had moved and was still trembling. A glance confirmed it. Today the car was a subdued green, it had a crew of three young men. Were the men rotated like the cars? What would I prefer: always the same men or always new ones? I didn't know them, that is, yes, I did know one: the one who had recently got out and crossed the road towards me, although only to queue at the Bockwurst stand under my window, and had returned to the car with three Bockwursts on a big paper plate and with three white rolls in the pockets of his grey-green parka. To a *blue* car. This young gentleman or comrade had had dark hair, which was beginning to thin at the parting. I could see that from above. For a moment I had enjoyed the thought: it was possible I had noticed the incipient baldness of the young man even before his own wife, who perhaps never looked down at him so attentively. I had then imagined how the men huddled cosily together in their car; how they ate up the Bockwursts and didn't even shiver, because the engine was running quietly and kept them warm. But what did they drink with the sausages? Did they each bring a thermos flask of coffee with them, like other working men?

I wished that when it had begun, on those first cold November nights, I had immediately trusted my impulse and taken hot tea down to them. It could have become a habit; after all, personally we had nothing against one another: each of us did what had to be done. A conversation might have developed—not about official duties, heaven forbid!—but about the weather, about illnesses, family matters.

Once, I had drunk tea late at night in the dark room, standing at the window in front of which we put up the curtains the next day. Suddenly I had to switch on the light, step right up to the window and wave to them. They flashed their headlights three times. They had a sense of humour. I had gone to bed a little calmer, a little less depressed. Depressed? I had never wanted to admit that to myself.

The telephone. A friend. Hello, I said. No, he wasn't interrupting any important work.

'Why not?' he said reproachfully.

'Oh,' I said, 'I couldn't answer that question in a single sentence.'

'You can go right ahead and use several sentences.'

'To be taken down.'

'You underestimate their technical capacities,' he said.

'They'll be able to spare a tape-recorder for the two of us, surely!'

'What it all costs,' I said.

There followed the kind of laughter which had become a habit on such occasions: provocative, a little vain. And if no one was listening in? If we were striking thin air with our show of bravado? It would not make the least difference.

The way I sound, this morning.

Well, how do I sound then?

'Well,' said my friend, 'not exactly high. Or do my ears deceive me?'

'Oh,' I said, 'how could I be anything but high: you've just phoned me.'

We always talked around the true text like that. I had to think of the two or three occasions when the true text had slipped out, because I didn't have the strength to hold it back, and how his eyes, his voice, had changed then.

'How is H?' he asked now.

'Well,' I said, 'I can visit him in the afternoons.'

'And we, madam, when shall we see one another?' he asked.

I spoke the true text: 'As soon as possible.'

He said he would be in town in the next few days and would let me know beforehand when to put on the water for coffee. He said this so that certain personnel highly valued by both of us could go ahead and rack their brains to work out what 'water for coffee' might mean.

I did not particularly like this kind of joke. 'Coffee? I thought you preferred tea.'

'Not at all.'

'*Bon*,' I said.

And he, after a short pause, his voice unchanged, 'You've got visitors, haven't you?'

I didn't like these questions either, but said, yes, incapable of lying.

'Well, wonderful,' said my friend. 'So I'll see you soon.'

Then I suddenly heard myself calling loudly into the telephone. 'You! Listen! One day we'll be old, remember that!'

He had hung up. But I sat down at my desk again and covered my face with my hands. I didn't cry. If I really thought about it, I had not cried for quite a long time.

Although I had not done any work, now, in the middle of my working hours, I would go shopping. It was a victory for them, I did not deceive myself about that, for if there was an ethic I held to then it was a work ethic, not least because it seemed capable of balancing out failings in other moral systems. I did not want to give up as those young gentlemen outside had given up, when they had allowed themselves—perhaps out of an inclination to conformity—to be hired for such an inexcusable idleness instead of doing proper work.

What now? Cause other people to rack their brains again? Slip on shoes, coat, double-lock the door, I would like to triple-lock it if I could, though I well knew how little good that would do, for at least once, probably twice in the previous summer those young gentlemen or their colleagues with a special training in door opening had visited the flat in my absence? One day the rubber sole of a man's shoe, size 41/42, had clearly imprinted itself on some door sills and on the dark floorboards in the middle room. And on another occasion the broken pieces of the bathroom wall mirror were lying in the sink, without there being any natural explanation for this circumstance. It seemed that the young gentlemen were not trying to conceal their visit to the flat at all.

One could call it intimidation, said an acquaintance who claimed to be very well informed, but were we intimidated? Of course we talked to others very quietly in the flat; if certain subjects arose (and they always came up) I turned the radio up loud, and sometimes we pulled the telephone wire out of the socket if we had guests, yet we remained aware that the measures the others took and our own reactions to them interlocked like the teeth of a good zip-fastener.

I stepped out into the street. Were they still there? They were there. Would they follow me? They did not follow me. According to my informed acquaintance I had been assigned the lowest grade of surveillance, warning surveillance, which meant conspicuous presence. A different grade would track every step with one, two, up to six cars (what it all cost!) when the subject to be observed was seriously suspected of a crime. Presumably this did not apply to us? The informed person shrugged his shoulders: it was conceivable that two different forms of surveillance could be brought to bear on one subject.

They might follow me on foot, but I could not discover a suspect in the window of the cosmetic shop. With a slight sense of dismay I observed myself breathe a sigh of relief. A specialist in Russian literature had assured me that Akhmatova had had a personal companion for twenty years. I now imagined this as, unfollowed and unaccompanied, I walked down Friedrichstrasse like an ordinary person and had to ask myself by what right I had earned this privilege. An idea began to dawn in me of what a strict and absolute kind of freedom there may be at the inmost centre of complete encirclement.

I always liked crossing the Weidendamm Bridge. Leaning over the parapet, I saw the ducks and seagulls, a barge with a black-red-gold flag. There was a wind, as usual. At the apex of the bridge hangs a cast-iron Prussian eagle; I lightly brushed it with my hand as I passed and it looked at me mockingly. Thinking nothing, I walked the few steps along the low stone balustrade, which is interrupted by the path to the door of that glass pavilion—popularly called 'the bunker of tears'—in which, in a light falling from narrow windows very high up, reflected by greenish tiled walls, the transformation of citizens of various states, including my state, into those in transit, tourists, those entering and those leaving, was executed. If the appearance of this building had corresponded with its purpose it would have been a monster, and not an ordinary building of stone, glass and iron struts, surrounded by well-cared-for grass, on which, of course, it was forbidden to walk. I had been forced to learn to be suspicious of these cared-for objects too, had understood that they all belonged to the master, who ruled my city unchallenged.

I needed to talk to someone. There was a little off-licence under the Friedrichstrasse elevated railway bridge. The sales assistant, an older woman with thin dyed hair, seemed to have been waiting only for me. She simply began a conversation about the pink champagne, which she actually had in stock and whose quality by no means every customer appreciated. She fetched a second bottle from the shelf for me.

Had she been working here for a long time? Oh, her whole life. Here or hereabouts. She was a native Berliner. Then she must have quite a lot of stories to tell.

Oh, once she got going! The most curious things had happened right in front of her eyes. The woman loved the word 'curious' and repeated it. I asked myself whether I was capable of listening to yet more curious stories, but something about this woman surprised me and I made as if I was interested. She was still attached to her Jewish friend with whom, as a girl, she had travelled on the elevated railway from Alex to Kudamm every morning: she was an apprentice in the department store, the friend (Elfriede was her name, Elfi) worked in the bank adding figures. Adding figures bored Elfi. When was that? Thirty-five, thirty-six . . . You needn't look surprised. Elfi's friend, an SS officer, had offered to get her out, but she had said only if my family gets out too. The guy was crazy about her. Well obviously it couldn't turn out well, but one's always wise after the event. He must have sorted something out for her after all—Holland was mentioned—and that's when they must have caught on to him. In any case, one fine day, as we came round the corner of Joachimsthaler Strasse—where he always waited for Elfi in his car so that he at least got one glance at her each day—there was his car, but as we passed we saw it was full of gentlemen with these trench coats and these little sports hats and Elfi's SS friend sitting at the wheel staring woodenly straight in front of him. I whispered through my teeth to Elfi: don't turn round. Just look straight in front of you and don't run! We carried it off. Well, we never heard anything else from that guy either. One can't have everything: perhaps he knew that. Thirty marks, the champagne.

The woman did not want to say anything more; I had to ask. Elfi? Then they took her away too of course. Forty-two, when they took away the last batch of Jews from Berlin. With her whole family. I never found a friend like her again, one becomes choosy. These things go round and round one's head for decades. We could have hidden her when it came to it. But a whole family?

All madness, she added as I was leaving, when I think back like this, pure madness.

I didn't want to go back home right away. I stared blindly at the window displays of the railway station bookshop, circled the newspaper kiosk, before going to the post office to withdraw some money. Someone who had known me would have recognized how edgy I was. Everything seemed to be taking too long, although at the same time I had to ask myself where I wanted to go to so quickly, why it was that I was in such a hurry. The attraction of uncertainty, on which one can become as dependent as on a drug. In the post office I saw an old acquaintance, and he saw me. Our eyes had met for a fraction of a second, but Jürgen M did not want to know me, his gaze had withdrawn more quickly than mine in fractions of fractions of seconds. How well I knew the curtain that drops down in front of the friend's gaze; the fish scales that draw across the white of the eyes; the cloud that obscures his lens: we haven't seen one another, never knew one another. It's better like that. One simply does one's business at another window. One can be ostentatiously engrossed with the documents which have to be shown to the girl behind the counter; one can take time over unnecessary forms. But Jürgen M shouldn't worry: I'm playing along. I'm already outside. It doesn't cross my mind to turn round.

Since when did I not go up to an old acquaintance without being sure that he wanted to meet me? Since when was I no longer the first to put out my hand to someone? To begin conversation? Since when had I held myself back? Prize question: how many people have to cross to the other side of the road at the sight of you, earnestly stare at the nearest shop-window display, change seats in the restaurant, turn their back to you at the meeting, before you behave accordingly? How often must you think 'accident' before you are ready to think 'intention'? I had to grin because I'm always pleased when I discover once again that statistics cannot answer real questions.

No loss, I thought. Jürgen M was no loss, so why did I care if he avoided me? Why did it bother me every time? Why doesn't one become steeled against it? What in me was not working? What mechanism was not intact? All right, everything in the right order now, and without rushing: Jürgen M. When was the last time I had seen Jürgen M? Many years ago, that much is certain. The occasion can't have been unpleasant. I'd teased him about the loud pattern of his tie. With a mocking bow he had handed me the glass of champagne that he had just taken from a tray, fetched himself a new one and touched my glass with his. Long time no see. He wanted to know whether I liked the pictures; I answered, partly. It was the opening of an exhibition in the old royal stables, things were not going too badly at the time, people who hadn't seen each other for a long time met and interrogated one another about the circumstances of their lives, as if they had spent the previous years in different countries. We had spent the previous years in different countries. As always, if it was reasonably possible, I kept to the rules of the game and asked Jürgen M how he passed his days. 'Me?' he said. 'Oh, you know. One gets through somehow.'

He had not said more than that, if I think carefully. Jürgen M, friend of the girl-friend of my student days, for whom a glittering future was predicted. Jürgen M the philosopher. Hadn't he attracted attention with a couple of explosive articles? By that time, it occurred to me, he was slimmer, wore his hair parted and had stopped being the friend of the girl-friend long before; I had first lost sight of him, then of her. Did he still publish in the relevant periodicals? Had the book, about which he had always talked non-stop, ever appeared? Had he failed, disappointed by himself and the world? Was that why he avoided meeting former acquaintances? So should I have gone up to him? But hadn't there been something else about Jürgen M?

S omeone came up behind me whistling so loudly and shrilly that it echoed in the underpass below the railway and could be heard above the noise of the traffic. I knew that song: '*To Karl Liebknecht we swore it, to Rosa Luxemburg we stretch out our hand.*' I wept. That had to stop. And it would stop unfortunately, probably very soon. The man who was whistling the song, a broad, heavy man of about forty, was wearing a black corduroy suit like carpenters wear; he strolled along, straddle-legged, whistling, unconcerned whether people turned around to look at him, as far as the door of the little café, through which he disappeared.

Could I imagine a woman to go with this man? I couldn't. It's usually women I can't imagine partners for; this time it was the other way round. The man was an exception. I could without any effort imagine a woman to go with Jürgen M, one of these superior mediocre women, because from my girl-friend, who had been difficult but also something special, he could only have gone to a mediocre woman. Or had my girl-friend left him? Had it not been altogether somewhat puzzling to all of us why the two had parted, after all those years?

Damn it all again, why on earth bother with Jürgen M? Had he not, at a time as tense as the present one, written that repulsive article attacking his professor! That was just like me, to have forgotten that and to have broken my resolution not to talk to him again. To have accosted him at the exhibition about that silly tie and then still be surprised at how zealously he had fetched me champagne! He'd been relieved that I'd spoken to him at all. But now things were not going well again and Jürgen M could easily afford not to know me. More than that perhaps: he wasn't *allowed* to talk to me. Maybe he even knew that . . .

Everything in the right order. And without rushing. What might he know? What *could* a man like Jürgen M know, beyond what he learned from the meagre public statements and the luxuriant rumours? Perhaps that was enough for him. Nevertheless, apart from my friends someone else must have been aware that there were young gentlemen outside my door: the person, for example, who had stationed them there.

There it was again, my obsession. I recognized it at once, yet had to plunge indulgently into it: that there must be someone who, apart from the really important things, knew everything about me. All the information—from the young gentlemen, from the telephone surveillance, from the postal surveillance—had to come together on some desk somewhere, in someone's head. What if it was in the skull of Jürgen M?

There seemed to be some degree of probability to that

thought, for my second involuntary thought was: then at last he would have what he wanted. This second thought astonished me. Since when did I have anything against Jürgen M? Since when did I think I knew what he needed? What else had I stored up, without even noticing it, about Jürgen M? Jürgen M as speaker—true, there had been that too. Before or after the business with the professor? I no longer knew. He'd had a reputation for openness, but to me everything he'd said was like a justification for earlier or future actions. I remember how fascinated many of our colleagues were by Jürgen M: at last someone who says how it really is. He received loud applause I remembered, and I, very depressed, wanted to go home quickly, but he waited for me at the door and dragged me along to the pub. It turned out to be a large party, a long evening. I hadn't known that Jürgen M drank. When he began to speak too loudly I made the mistake of asking him: why do you drink? He swung his head round to me, as if I had struck him. 'Always so superior, madam!' he said. That man hated me. 'Have I done something to you?' I asked helplessly, and that one sentence broke down a dam which Jürgen M had thrown up around himself and a confession flowed unstoppably out of him. I had to listen and didn't want to listen because I knew: afterwards he will not only hate me; afterwards he'll be dangerous. But I was caught in the spell of his rage and of my own curiosity and so I had learned then that he, Jürgen M, had been following my life for years. That he knew every word that I had said or written, and more than that every word that I had refused to use. He knew my circumstances—if an outsider can know the circumstances of another person at all—he had thought, felt, his way into me with an intensity that dumbfounded me. He believed me—this roused him to white heat—to be successful and happy. And arrogant, that above all. 'Arrogant,' I asked foolishly, 'in what way?' Because I seemed to believe one could have everything without selling one's soul for it. 'But I ask you,' I said, if only to break through the oppressiveness, 'we aren't living in the Middle Ages any more!' Now he really got going. Not in the Middle Ages! There you have it: that was just what I thought I could believe, presumably even really believed, and was not only, as he had thought for a long time, artfully holding it in front of me as a standard, in order to take advantage of everything behind it. 'All your lack of realism,' said Jürgen M, 'this playing about on the high wire without falling off.' But now, just between the two of us, he's going to open my eyes for me. Not in the Middle Ages? Oh yes, madam. We *are* in the Middle Ages. Nothing has changed, only appearances. Nothing will change. And if one wants to raise oneself above the ignorant mass as an initiate then one must sell one's soul just as one always had to. And if I really wanted to know, blood still flows too, even if not one's own. Not always one's own.

Now I knew again, what I suddenly realized then: they had him in their grasp. And I remembered that my arrogance—he may have been right about that, talented psychologist that he was—caused me to ask him quietly: why don't you get out? And how he turned white as the wall, opened his eyes wide, brought his face close to mine so that I smelt his beer breath and utterly soberly said three words: I—am—afraid. After that he immediately played the drunk again; I stood up, tapped the table and left. After that I didn't see Jürgen M for years, had forgotten the scene, which he will never forget, and now he doesn't need to know me but sits in the building with the many telephones and collects to his heart's delight all the information about me that no one else could obtain, and every morning thanks fate for having placed him in this position in which he can satisfy his passionate desires and be useful to society at the same time.

Like I am, in my place.

I ran blindly across the Weidendamm Bridge to the other side and in the opposite direction. The files would have to be selected, formulated, possibly dictated to a secretary. Or how should one imagine it? Should I imagine that Jürgen M entered his office punctually at eight in the morning and as his first act—I granted my imagination this vanity—reached for the slim dossier carrying my name? In it the previous day's report on which Jürgen M concentrated indulgently. Aha. Yesterday—that was today—she conducted a telephone conversation at nine-forty-five. Caller: the name of my friend. Followed by the text of our conversation, over which Jürgen M, who could now certainly allow himself some humour, would smirk. He would allow himself contempt too. 'Coffee', 'tea'—oh you poor amateurs! Jürgen M was a professional if I imagined him correctly and, intelligent as he was, he must nevertheless inevitably be gripped—one fine morning while reading the daily report from his informants—by the futility of his actions, because if he leafed through all the files, read a line here, a shorthand report or a record of a conversation there, and if he then asked himself what he now knew about these objects that he had not known before, then he honestly had to say to himself: nothing. And if he would further ask himself what he had achieved, he would have to say to himself yet again: nothing.

I knew better. He had achieved a lot, the good man, quite a lot, but he could not know what because his informers hadn't heard it, his tapes hadn't recorded it, it is of too fine a stuff, it gives them the slip, even the finest net doesn't catch it, and if I now asked myself what this mysterious 'it' really was then I too had no name for it. Dissatisfied with myself and unable to approve what I now intended to do, I walked across the car park, headed towards the bottle-green car (they were still there, what else had I expected?). It was eleven-fifteen, I passed very close to the car and caught the three young gentlemen at their breakfast. The one sitting behind the steering-wheel had his sandwich-box on his knees, the one beside him was biting into an apple and the one behind in the back was taking a long drink from a bottle of bitter lemon. He didn't choke as my face appeared in front of him, he calmly went on drinking, but as if at a word of command all three assumed the glazed look. Maybe, I said to myself—as for the sake of decency I walked diagonally across the car park to the letter-box, as if I had some things to post, and even went as far as to feign dropping things in—maybe they learn this glazed look at their school. Apart from social sciences they also have to learn practical skills, after all. And it may be, in the second year of their course that on their timetable once a week is: training in the glazed look.

And if it isn't Jürgen M at all, but someone else? I knew that voice. A good day to you, dear self-censor, haven't heard from you for a long time. So who should it be, if not Jürgen M, in your opinion?—An impartial official, who doesn't know you at all.—I would even prefer that.—Prefer is good.—Anyway. One who doesn't have any personal interest in me. Who doesn't want to get the better of me in my very own field.

Like Jürgen M? Get a hold of yourself!

From experience I knew that inner dialogue is preferable to permanent inner monologue. So I asked my inner censor to consider what presumably drove Jürgen M on: namely that he was intent on proving to me that not only a writer can find out everything about a person. He could do it too in his own way. He too could, like any author, make himself lord and master over his subjects. But since his subjects are of flesh and blood and do not, like mine, stay on paper, *he* is the true master, the real lord.

And so, do you—said the unwelcome voice, which can be very tactless—want to compete with him? Want to take up the gauntlet? Show him who the master is? Then he has already won, your clean Jürgen M.

But what else should I do, I asked myself as I unlocked the letter-box in the hallway, took out post and newspapers, what should I do? Up the stairs, towards the hall mirror, which has not yet been broken. That I was pale didn't mean anything; I was just short of breath; the voice wished me joy in my middle age and I called it impertinent. Besides, had there not been something pitiable about the lemonade-drinking young man in the car downstairs?—I should not trivialize an undignified occurrence. So dignity was still an issue? Still? Who could tell us what dignity is?

I looked at my post after the usual preliminaries; after I had satisfied myself that there were no disagreeable senders among them, none, which alarmed me. After I had held the envelopes up to the light until that shiny border of glue was revealed which evidently resulted from the second sealing. It was much rarer for the gummed edges of the envelopes to be more ridged than usual, and only occasionally did I find the letter paper sticking to the envelope: such mistakes should be avoidable. Somewhere—presumably not even somewhere hidden—there must be a huge building (or were there smaller houses in every district?), to which vanloads of mail were delivered every day, which were then sorted at a long conveyer-belt by diligent women's hands and in accordance with points of view opaque to us were passed up to the higher storeys, where once again women (carefully, carefully) opened the letters over steam—or were there more effective methods now?—and brought them to the holy of holies, where skilled colleagues were able to make use of the photocopy machines, which we so lacked in our libraries and publishing houses. An army of employees, who would never ever receive an appreciation in the press; to whom no day of the year was dedicated, like the miners, the teachers or the staff of the health service. An ever-expanding band who had to reconcile themselves to operating in the dark. I saw crowds of people disappearing from view into deep shadow. Their fate did not seem enviable to me.

I laid the newspapers aside after I had skimmed over the headlines. I had still not opened three letters. I knew who they were from although on one there was neither a sender nor a postage stamp: the sender, a very young poet, was in the habit of putting his letters in my house letter-box himself. I had never ever seen him. From his poems—the new ones had been written in a pre-military training camp—I imagined a delicate quiet boy with gentle blue eyes, who suffered without being able to defend himself and survived by writing poems; I read this boy's poems reluctantly, because I could not help him. My letters to him were evasive and I was sometimes angry at him, even more at myself. He could be my son. I thought I could foresee what was waiting for him. They ran on to the knife blade. The young gentlemen who sat outside my door—they would simply walk through his: that was the difference between the two of us—a decisive difference. A ditch. Did I have to jump over it?

Translated from the German by Martin Chalmers.

RYSZARD KAPUŚCIŃSKI

BOLIVIA, 1970

There is a demonstration on the other side of La Paz. People dressed in black gather in front of the university: students, mothers and fathers, sisters and brothers, wives and children of those who have died at Teoponte. They move in a procession toward the Miraflores district, where the General Staff Office is. They pass through the narrow streets of the old town, which rise steeply or drop precipitously. In all of La Paz there is not one level street. Walking around is exhausting.

People know what happened in Teoponte and what sort of procession they are in. They stop and remove their caps, and the God-fearing Indians kneel on the sidewalks. Maria Cecilia holds the arm of Maria Luisa, who lost three sons on one day. I walk at the end of the procession, because I want to see what will happen.

The sentries at the General Staff Office admit us without a word, because the people in black have been coming there every day for a month, and there is a standing order to admit them. We enter a room in the main building where, for a month, the same performance has taken place every day. The families sit on benches, and the commander of the army enters to hear their appeal. They want the army to turn over the bodies of the fallen. The commander of the army answers that this is impossible for security reasons. Of course there no security reasons. The commander maintains that all the partisans died in battle. In fact they were shot in the back of the head as soon as they surrendered. The bodies constitute evidence of a crime, and that is not what the army wants.

This time, in the General Staff Office, there is great confusion. Weapons have been thrown on tables, papers dumped in the corridors. The mess is from the military coup that just ended. The coup did not last long. The military radio station in La Paz broadcast a communiqué that the army was demanding the resignation of the president of the republic, general Alfredo Ovando. Ovando was sleeping peacefully in the city of Santa Cruz, 1,000 kilometres east of La Paz. He was awakened and told the bad news. The president decided to await further developments. Nothing happened for several hours because the rebels, led by the army general Rogelio Miranda, had decided to wait in La Paz and see what the president would do. Ovando was waiting in Santa Cruz and Miranda was waiting in La Paz. Both knew the rules of the *coup d'état* game well.

Ovando had overthrown two presidents: Paz Estenssoro in 1964 and Adolfo Silesa five years later. Ovando had been president for a year. He had begun as a leftish politician, nationalizing the local branch of Gulf Oil and restoring the legality of trade unions. It was said that by these actions he wanted to erase a painful item from his biography: he had given the order to finish off the wounded Che Guevara. He was a feebly built man with an anxious face. He did not smile and would go for days without speaking. Perhaps he felt he had nothing to say. Having catered to the left for six months, Ovando started over the next six months to cater to the right. He did not cater enough to the right, however, because the right decided to remove him.

Ovando returned to La Paz in the afternoon. His airplane landed at the El Alto military airbase, 4,100 metres above sea-level on a great desert plateau. The plateau ends abruptly in a cliff. At the bottom of the cliff lies La Paz. Whoever controls El Alto has a good chance of controlling La Paz, since it is easy to shell the city from the edge of the cliff.

A *coup d'état* contains many elements of spectacle. Ovando was greeted by General Juan Torres, the former defence minister in the Ovando government, whom the president had removed to placate the right. Many air force officers greeted him; the air force had declined to take part in the coup. He drove to the presidential palace and made a speech from the balcony. The balcony overlooks the main square, known as Plaza Murillo. The square was crowded with people. They had learned about the military coup and had come to watch the show. An orchestra played in the centre of the square. At the sight of the general, the orchestra broke off; Ovando announced, more or less, that he was still and would remain president. He appealed to the army for common sense and to the people for unity. Some applauded and others whistled their dissatisfaction that nothing had changed.

Ovando returned to his office and placed a telephone call to Miranda, who as commander of the army was sitting in his room at the General Staff Office. They agreed to hold talks on neutral ground, at the papal nuncio's residence.

The talks began at midnight. At three in the morning Miranda came to his senses and realized that Ovando was accompanied by a powerful escort, while he himself had brought only a few officers. Ovando could lock him up! He demanded a recess, drove to the General Staff Office and returned an hour later surrounded by a platoon of bully boys armed to the teeth. The talks resumed.

At six in the morning (it was a Monday), they concluded the following pact: both of them, the president of the republic and the commander of the army, would offer to resign. Officers at La Paz garrison would vote on the matter. If they voted for resignation, the president and the commander would step down; if the officers voted against, they would resume their talks and seek another way out.

The officers assembled at three in the afternoon. In a secret ballot, 317 voted for resignation and forty against.

Ovando ignored the result. Two hours later, he appeared on the balcony of the palace and told the waiting crowd that, as president of the republic, he was removing General Miranda from his post as commander of the army. The army split. Some took Ovando's side, and some Miranda's. Opposing factions loaded their weapons, warming up the engines of their tanks and aircraft. War hung in the air.

Ovando did not have the mental strength to hold out long enough. He feared bloodshed and decided to back down, even though a majority of the garrisons stood behind him. All through Monday night and into Tuesday a dramatic cabinet meeting took place in Ovando's residence. The ministers urged him to stay on, but Ovando kept repeating: No, no. He wanted peace; he wanted to be ambassador in Madrid. Ovando was a neurasthenic, and this decisive night found him in a defeatist mood that he was unable to control. At six in the morning he adjourned the cabinet meeting, wrote a letter of resignation, got into his car and drove to the Argentine embassy to ask for asylum.

Meanwhile, another car was speeding towards El Alto. General Juan Torres was inside. At the base, air force officers faithful to the government (which no longer existed) and representatives of the Workers' Central and the Students' Federation were waiting for him. A council was held. Torres was unanimously chosen Provisional President of the Revolutionary Government of Bolivia.

But they were not asleep at the General Staff Office either. At the news of Ovando's resignation, general Miranda called a meeting of the rebels, who elected him President of the Republic. Bolivia now had two presidents: Torres and Miranda.

Each president disposed of part of the army. A head-on collision would bring about a bloodbath and the dissolution of the army. Neither Torres nor Miranda wanted this; they were generals and they leaned on the army.

A wise person once said that in politics you don't have to do anything, because half the problems cannot be solved anyway, and half solve themselves. In politics, you have to know how to wait. Who waits better, wins. Torres waited (at El Alto) and Miranda waited (at the General Staff Office). Miranda came out of the coup looking the more strange. He had created the problem by announcing the coup in the first place, but did not know what to do next. Miranda did not possess a great intellect. He did not know how to connect facts; he was not capable of thinking. He paced around the staff office, wrinkling his brows.

The rebels, who had trusted their commander, did not know what to do either. They had supported Miranda's coup, elected him president, but nothing had changed. No order had been given to occupy the palace or to form a government. Murmuring arose in the ranks of the rebels. Miranda was still figuring, racking his brains, pressing his temples, but no strategy emerged. He was not thinking but, more importantly, he was not acting.

The officers of the garrison called a meeting at which they decided to name a presidential triumvirate made up of the commanders of the three branches of the armed forces. The triumvirate included General Efrain Guachalla (army), General

Fernando Sattori (air force) and Rear-Admiral Alberto Albarracin (navy). They were sworn in on Tuesday at noon in the Presidential Palace.

On Tuesday morning, Bolivia had two presidents (Torres and Miranda). On Tuesday afternoon it had three new presidents (Guachalla, Sattori and Albarracin). The afternoon presidents were sworn in and the morning presidents were not, so the legal standing of the afternoon presidents was better and the morning presidents had to step down.

In fact, only Miranda resigned, to make way for the presidential troika. The presidents summoned a cabinet. They named eighteen cabinet ministers. The cabinet existed for a few hours. One of the presidents, General Sattori, drove to El Alto on Tuesday evening to hold talks with Torres. At three in the morning he announced his resignation and his backing of Torres. The two remaining presidents resigned two hours later. It was five o'clock on Wednesday morning.

Several minutes later Torres's man, the commander of the battalion for the protection of the government, Major Ruben Sanchez, occupied the Presidential Palace with his force. He telephoned El Alto Air Force Base.

'Mr President, the road to the palace is clear.'

At six in the morning, Torres left El Alto for the city. He rode in an open Jeep. A long column of vehicles followed, carrying soldiers from the units that supported him. Cheering crowds stood along the route. Residents of the poor Villa Victoria and Muyupampa districts stood there. Miners from Cartavi and Oruro. Peasants from Cochabamba and Santa Cruz. Students from San Andres. Torres rode along, tired after a sleepless night but smiling. He bowed and said, '*Muchas gracias,*' because these people had carried him to power. There had been a general strike throughout the country since Tuesday. There had been great demonstrations in support of Torres. Miranda and his rebels knew that they would not be able to take power. They had to give up. Miranda had resigned and asked for asylum in the Paraguayan embassy.

After arriving at the Presidential Palace, Torres made a speech from the balcony. A crowd of supporters filled the Plaza

Murillo and the whole downtown area. The people cheered amid an atmosphere of great festivity. Torres spoke about the revolution and dignity, about work and a better life. He said that the government would combat fascism, that the people would be free. A government of workers, peasants, students and soldiers would emerge. The crowd roared.

General Reque Teran, who under Torres became commander of the army, now speaks with the families of those who fell at Teoponte. He expresses understanding and promises to help. I look out of the window towards the residential district for army officers that adjoins the General Staff Office. Soldiers are loading baggage and furniture into trucks. It is moving-day. Every coup means a moving-day. Those who bet on the losers are headed for distant garrisons. Those who find themselves on the winning side move into more spacious quarters.

The meeting ends and everyone gets up to leave. Retired general Anastosio Villanueva, whose son died at Teoponte, approaches me.

'Are you a journalist?' he asks. He had seen me write in my notebook.

'Yes,' I answer.

'From where?' he asks.

'From Poland.'

'Ah, from Poland. Is this your first time in Bolivia?'

'No, my second.'

'Your second. So you do not know this country. We do not know it, either. There are those who say that this country should not exist. That Brazil could take part of it, Argentina another part, and Peru the rest. But this is our state, and once a state appears, it will continue to exist. Have you ever seen a state arise and then disappear? That is impossible.

'I think this is a hard country to understand. Do you know that Torres won thanks to those boys from Teoponte? Let me explain. When they found themselves in Teoponte there was an outcry that the government was permitting chaos, that it was permitting civil war. A government like that has to be removed

165

and a strong-arm administration formed. That is exactly what Miranda and his people, the whole right wing, said. They thought that everything would come easily; they did not prepare, they improvised.

'Among us Latinos, everything is improvised. The most important thing is to get started, and then take what God gives. But God seldom gives—I'm an old man, believe what I say. Do you know how many coups I've lived through? Perhaps twenty. You saw six changes of president in three days, simply because Miranda doesn't know how to think. Torres is an honest man. He comes from the poor. He never knew his father, and his mother is an Indian. I don't know what the left will do, but it has won. Torres is their man. But how long he'll be able to hold on, I do not know.'

Translated from the Polish by William Brand.

In July 1970, Chato Peredo, avenging the deaths of his two brothers, Coco and Inti—both killed for serving as guerrillas with Che Guevara in Bolivia—formed his own revolutionary army. It consisted of seventy-five men, mainly students; its goal was 'the victory of the revolution, the creation of a people's government and the nationalization of all wealth.' On the eighteenth, his unit set out into the Bolivian jungle and was promptly surrounded by the Bolivian army and, after being deprived of food and water, surrendered in the village of Teoponte. There were eight survivors. Twelve had died in the jungle. Fifty-five were shot by the army. Ryszard Kapuściński arrived in Bolivia a month later.

FERDINANDO SCIANNA

BOLIVIA, 1990

Ferdinando Scianna

The name of the camp where I took these photographs is Kami, which is also the name of the mountain to which it clings. Kami is a miners camp. The men who live here mine for tungsten in the Andes. The camp is near the entrance to the mine, at 11,400 feet.

Bolivians have been mining Kami since 1908. In the sixties, when tungsten was fetching high prices, 9,000 people lived in the camp. But in the early seventies prices fell; the mine became unsafe and difficult to work, and the government handed it over to a workers co-operative. Less than 6,000 people live here now, and more people than ever are leaving. Those miners and their families that have stayed live in shacks made of corrugated zinc.

Photographing these people I came to realize that their lives are dominated by fear: fear of old galleries falling, of dynamite, of the spirits trapped in the mine, of tuberculosis, of the disappearance of *veta* (the wolfram seam), of the future.

The co-operative is called *El Progresso*. I attended one of their general meetings. At the meeting a group of Italian volunteers proposed a project to search for gold. The project would take two years. It would be funded by the miners themselves at a rate that could only lead to starvation; the prospect of finding gold was very remote. The assembly voted in favour of the project.

ISABEL ALLENDE
GIFT FOR A SWEETHEART

H oracio Fortunato was forty-six when the languid Jewish woman who was to change his roguish ways and deflate his fanfaronade entered his life. Fortunato came from a long line of circus people, the kind who are born with rubber bones and a natural gift for somersaults, people who at an age when other infants are crawling around like worms are hanging upside down from a trapeze and brushing the lion's teeth. Before his father made it into a serious enterprise, rather than the idle fancy it had been, the Fortunato Circus experienced more difficulty than glory. At different times of catastrophe and turmoil the company was reduced to two or three members of the clan who wandered the byways in a broken-down gypsy wagon with a threadbare tent they set up in godforsaken little towns. For years Horacio's grandfather bore the sole responsibility for the spectacle: he walked the tightrope, juggled with lighted torches, swallowed Toledo-steel swords, extracted oranges and serpents from a top hat and danced a graceful minuet with a female monkey decked out in ruffles and a plumed hat. His grandfather, however, managed somehow to survive bad times and while many other circuses succumbed, obliterated by more modern diversions, he saved his circus and, at the end of his life, was able to retire to the south of the continent and cultivate his garden of asparagus and strawberries, leaving a debt-free enterprise to his son Fortunato II. The scion lacked his father's humility, nor was he disposed to perform a balancing act on a tightrope or do pirouettes with a chimpanzee; on the other hand, he was gifted with the unshakable prudence of a born businessman. Under his direction the circus grew in size and prestige until it was the largest in the nation. Three colossal striped tents replaced the modest tarp of the earlier hard times; various cages sheltered a travelling zoo of tamed wild animals; and other fanciful vehicles transported the artists, who included the only hermaphroditic and ventriloquist dwarf in history. An exact, wheeled replica of Christopher Columbus's caravan completed the Fortunato Family Famous International Circus. This enormous caravel no longer drifted aimlessly, as it had in his grandfather's day, but steamed purposefully along the principal highways from the Rio Grande to the Straits of Magellan, stopping only in major cities, where it made an entrance with such a clamour of drums, elephants and clowns—the caravel at the lead, like a miraculous re-enactment of the Conquest—that no man, woman or child could escape knowing the circus had come to town.

Fortunato II married a trapeze artist, and they had a son they named Horacio. But one day, wife-and-mother stayed behind, determined to be independent of her husband and support herself through her somewhat precarious calling, leaving the boy in his father's care. Her son held a rather dim picture of her in his memory, never completely separating the image of his mother from that of the many acrobats he had known. When he was ten, his father married another circus artist, this time an equestrienne able to stand on her head on a galloping steed or leap from one croup to another with eyes blindfolded. She was very beautiful. But no matter how much soap, water and perfume she used, she could not erase the last trace of the essence of horse, a sharp aroma of sweat and effort. In her magnificent bosom, the young Horacio, enveloped in that unique odour, found consolation for his mother's absence. But with time, the horsewoman also decamped without a farewell. In the ripeness of his years, Fortunato II entered into matrimony, for the third and final time, with a Swiss woman he met on a tour bus in America. He was weary of his Bedouin-like existence and felt too old for new alarms, so when his Swiss bride requested it, he had not the slightest difficulty in giving up the circus for a sedentary life and ended his days on a small farm in the Alps amid bucolic hills and woods. His son Horacio, who was a little over twenty, took charge of the family business.

Horacio had grown up with the instability of moving every few days, of sleeping on wheels and living beneath a canvas roof, but he was very content with his fate. He had never envied other little boys who wore grey uniforms to school and had their destinies mapped out before they were born. By contrast, he felt powerful and free. He knew all the secrets of the circus, and with the same confidence and ease he mucked out the animal cages or balanced fifty metres above the ground dressed as a hussar, charming the audience with his dolphin smile. If at any moment he longed for stability, he did not admit it, even in his sleep. The experience of having been abandoned first by his mother and then by his step-mother had left him slightly insecure, especially with women, but it had not made him a cynic, because he had inherited his grandfather's sentimental heart. He had an enormous flair for the circus, but he was fascinated by the commercial aspect of the business even more than by the art. He had intended to be rich from the time he was a young boy, with the naïve conviction that money would bring the security he had not had with his family. He increased the number of tentacles spreading from the family enterprise by buying a chain of boxing arenas in several capital cities. From boxing he moved naturally to wrestling and as he was a man of inventive imagination he transformed that gross sport into a dramatic spectacle. Among his initiatives were the Mummy, who appeared at ringside in an Egyptian sarcophagus; Tarzan, who covered his privates with a tiger skin so tiny that with every lunge the audience held its breath, expecting some major revelation; and the Angel, who every night bet his golden hair and lost it to the scissors of the ferocious Kuramoto—a Mapuche Indian disguised as a Samurai—but then appeared the following day with curls intact, irrefutable proof of his divine condition. These and other commercial ventures, along with public appearances with a pair of bodyguards whose role it was to intimidate his competitors and pique the ladies' curiosity, had earned him the reputation of being a shady character, a distinction he revelled in. He lived a good life, travelled through the world closing deals and looking for monsters, frequented clubs and casinos, owned a glass mansion in California and a retreat in the Yucatán, but lived most of the year in luxury hotels. He bought the temporary company of a series of blondes. He liked them soft, with ample bosoms, in homage to the memory of his stepmother, but he wasted very little energy on amorous affairs and when his grandfather urged him to marry and bring sons into the world so the Fortunato name would not vanish without an heir, he replied that not even out of his mind would he ascend the matrimonial gallows. He was a dark-skinned, hefty man with thick hair slicked back with brilliantine, shrewd eyes and an authoritative voice that accentuated his self-satisfied vulgarity. He was obsessed with elegance and he bought clothes befitting a duke—but his suits were a little too shiny; his ties verging on the audacious; the ruby in his ring too ostentatious; his cologne too penetrating. He had the heart of a lion tamer, and no English tailor alive would ever disguise that fact.

This man, who had spent a good part of his existence cutting a wide swathe with his lavish lifestyle, met Patricia Zimmerman on a Tuesday in March and on the spot lost both unpredictability of spirit and clarity of thought. He was sitting in the only restaurant in the city that still refused to serve blacks, with four cohorts and a diva whom he was planning to take to the Bahamas for a week, when Patricia entered the room on her husband's arm, dressed in silk and adorned with some of the diamonds that had made the Zimmerman firm famous. Nothing could be further from the unforgettable stepmother smelling of horses, or the complacent blondes, than this woman. He watched her advance, small, refined, her chest-bones bared by her *décolletage* and her chestnut-coloured hair drawn back into a severe bun, and he felt his knees grow heavy and an insufferable burning in his breast. He preferred uncomplicated women ready for a good time, whereas this was a woman who would have to be studied carefully if her worth were to be known, and even then her virtues would be visible only to an eye trained in appreciating subtleties—which had never been the case with Horacio Fortunato. If the fortune-teller in his circus had consulted her crystal ball and predicted that Fortunato would fall in love at first sight with a fortyish and haughty aristocrat, he would have had a good laugh. But that is exactly what happened as he watched Patricia walk toward him like the shade of a nineteenth-century widow-empress in her dark gown with the glitter of all those diamonds shooting fire at her neck. As Patricia walked past, she paused for an instant before that giant with the napkin tucked into his waistcoat and a trace of gravy at the corner of his mouth. Horacio Fortunato caught a whiff of her perfume and the full impact of her aquiline profile and completely forgot the diva, the bodyguards, his business affairs, everything that interested him in life and decided with absolute seriousness to steal this woman from her jeweller and love her to the best of his ability. He turned his chair to one side and, ignoring his guests, measured the distance that separated her from him, while Patricia Zimmerman wondered whether that stranger was examining her jewels with some evil design.

That same night an extravagant bouquet of orchids was delivered to the Zimmerman residence. Patricia looked at the card, a sepia-coloured rectangle with a name from a novel written in golden arabesques. What ghastly taste, she muttered, divining immediately it had come from the man with the plastered-down hair she had seen in the restaurant, and she ordered that the gift be tossed into the street. The following day a crystal box arrived bearing a single perfect rose, without a card. The major-domo also placed this offering in the trash. Different bouquets followed for the rest of the week: a basket of wild flowers on a bed of lavender, a pyramid of white carnations in a silver goblet, a dozen black tulips imported from Holland and other blooms impossible to find in this hot climate. Each suffered the fate of the first, but this did not discourage the gallant, whose siege was becoming so unbearable that Patricia Zimmerman did not dare answer the telephone for fear of hearing his voice whispering indecent proposals, as had happened the previous Tuesday at two in the morning. She returned his letters unopened. She stopped going out because she ran into Fortunato in the most unexpected places: observing her from the adjoining box at the opera; in the street, waiting to open the door of her car before the chauffeur could reach it; materializing like an illusion in an elevator or on some stairway. She was a prisoner in her own home, and frightened. He'll get over it, he'll get over it, she kept telling herself, but Fortunato did not evaporate like a bad dream; he was always there, on the other side of the wall, breathing heavily. She thought of calling the police or telling her husband, but her horror of scandal prevented her. One morning she was attending to her correspondence when the major-domo announced the visit of the President of Fortunato and Sons.

'In my own house, how dare he!' Patricia muttered, her heart racing. She had to call on the implacable discipline she had acquired in years of small dramas played in salons to disguise the trembling of her hands and voice. For an instant, she was tempted to confront this madman once and for all, but she realized that her strength would fail her; she felt defeated even before she saw him.

'Tell him I'm not in. Show him the door and inform the servants that the gentleman is not welcome in this house,' she ordered.

The next day there were no exotic flowers at breakfast, and Patricia thought, with a sigh of relief or dejection, that the man must finally have understood her message. That morning she felt free for the first time in a week, and she went out for a game of tennis and a visit to the beauty salon. She returned home at two in the afternoon with a new haircut and a bad headache. On the hall table she saw a royal purple velvet jewel box with the name Zimmerman printed in gold letters. She opened it rather absently, thinking that her husband had left it there, but found a necklace of emeralds accompanied by one of those pretentious sepia cards she had come to know and detest. Her headache turned to panic. This adventurer seemed prepared to ruin her life; as if it weren't enough to buy a necklace from her own husband, he then had the gall to send it to her house. She could not throw this gift into the trash, as she had done with the flowers. With the case clutched to her bosom, she locked herself in her writing-room. A half-hour later, she called the chauffeur and ordered him to deliver a package to the same address to which he had returned several letters. As she handed him the jewels she felt no relief; to the contrary, she had the impression that she was sinking into a quagmire.

At the same time, Fortunato was slogging through his own swamp, getting nowhere, feeling his way blindly. He had never spent so much money and time to court a woman, although it was true, he admitted, that all his women had been quite different from this one. For the first time in his life as a showman, he felt ridiculous. He could not go on this way; always strong as an ox, his health was suffering; he slept only a few hours at a time; he was short of breath; he had heart palpitations; he felt fire in his stomach and ringing in his temples. His business was similarly suffering the impact of his love fever; he was making hasty decisions, and losing money. Good Christ, I don't know who I am or what I'm doing here; damn it all, he grumbled, sweating, but not for a minute did he consider abandoning the chase.

Slumped in an armchair in the hotel where he was staying, the purple jewel box back in his hands, Fortunato remembered his grandfather. Horacio rarely thought of his father, but his memory often dwelt on that formidable ancestor who at ninety-some years was still cultivating his garden. He picked up the telephone and asked for long distance.

The elder Fortunato was nearly deaf and, in addition, unable to adapt to the mechanism of that devilish apparatus that carried voices halfway around the planet, but the years had not affected his lucidity. He listened carefully to his grandson's sorrowful tale, speaking only at the end.

'So, the sly vixen is giving herself the luxury of snubbing my boy, is that it, eh?'

'She won't even look at me, Nono. She's rich, she's beautiful, she's classy . . . she has everything.'

'Ummm . . . including a husband.'

'Yes, but that's not important. If I could only speak to her.'

'Speak to her? What about? You have nothing to say to a woman like that, son.'

'I gave her a necklace fit for a queen and she returned it without a word.'

'Well, give her something she doesn't have.'

'What, for example?'

'A good excuse to laugh, that always gets 'em,' and his grandfather nodded off with the receiver in his hand, dreaming of the pretty things who had given him their hearts as he performed his death-defying acrobatics on the trapeze or danced with his monkey.

The next day in his office the jeweller Zimmerman received a splendid young woman, a manicurist by trade, she said; she had come on behalf of the purchaser, she explained, to sell back at half price the very emerald necklace he had sold only forty-eight hours before. The jeweller remembered the purchaser very well: impossible to forget such a conceited boor.

'I need something that will crumble the defences of a haughty lady,' he had said.

Zimmerman remembered having studied him for a moment and deciding he must be one of those new oil or cocaine millionaires. He could not tolerate vulgarity; he was accustomed to a different class of customer. He rarely served clients himself, but this man had insisted on speaking to him and seemed prepared to spend an unlimited amount of money.

'What do you recommend?' the man had asked before the tray where the most valuable jewels sparkled.

'It depends upon the lady. Rubies and pearls look good on dark skin, emeralds on someone fairer and diamonds are perfect for anyone.'

'She has too many diamonds. Her husband gives them to her as if they were candy.'

Zimmerman coughed. He disliked this kind of confidence. The man picked up the necklace, held it to the light with no respect, shook it like a sleigh-bell, and the air filled with tinkling and green sparks as the jeweller's ulcer twitched within him.

'Do you think emeralds bring good luck?'

'I suppose that all precious stones fit that description, sir, but I am not superstitious.'

'This is a very special woman. I don't want to make any mistake with the gift, you understand?'

'Perfectly.'

But apparently that was precisely what had happened, Zimmerman told himself, unable to restrain a scornful smirk when the girl returned the necklace. No, there was nothing wrong with the jewels; the mistake was the girl. He had imagined a more refined woman, certainly not a manicurist carrying a plastic handbag and wearing a cheap blouse. He was, none the less, intrigued by the girl; there was something vulnerable and pathetic about her, poor child; she would not fare well in the hands of that bandit, he thought.

'Why don't you tell me the whole story, my dear,' said Zimmerman finally.

The girl spun him the tale she had memorized, and an hour

later left the shop with a light step. According to plan, the jeweller had not only bought back the necklace, he invited her to dinner as well. It was plain to her that Zimmerman was one of those men who are astute and suspicious in business dealings but naïve in every other regard; she would have no difficulty distracting him the amount of time Horacio Fortunato needed and was prepared to pay for.

That was a memorable night for Zimmerman; he had planned on dinner but found himself in the grip of an unexpected passion. The next day he saw his new friend again and by the end of the week he was stammering to Patricia something about going to New York for a few days to attend a sale of Russian jewels saved from the massacre of Ekaterimburg. His wife was totally unmoved.

Alone in her house, too listless to go out and suffering that headache that came and went without respite, Patricia decided to devote her Saturday to recouping her strength. She settled on the terrace to leaf through some fashion magazines. It had not rained for a week and the air was humid and hot. She read a while, until the sun made her drowsy; her body grew heavy, her eyes closed and the magazine slipped from her hands. At that moment she heard a sound from deep in the garden; she thought it must be the gardener, a headstrong old man who in less than a year had transformed her property into a tropical jungle, ripping out pots of chrysanthemums to make way for an efflorescence gone wild. She opened her eyes, stared half-seeing against the sun, and saw something unusually large moving in the top of the avocado tree. She removed her dark glasses and sat up. No doubt about it, a shadow was moving up there, and it was not part of the foliage.

Patricia Zimmerman rose from her chair and walked forward a step or two; then she saw it clearly: a ghostly blue-clad figure with a golden cape flew several metres over her head, turned a somersault in the air and, for an instant, seemed to freeze at the moment of waving to her from the sky. She choked back a scream, sure that the apparition would plummet like a stone and be pulverized on contact with the ground, but the cape filled with air and that gleaming coleopteran stretched out its arms and swung into a nearby medlar tree. Immediately, a second blue figure appeared, hanging by its legs in the top branches of another tree, swinging by the wrists a young girl wearing a flower crown. The first gave a signal and the holder released the girl, who scattered a rain of paper butterflies before being caught by the ankles. Patricia did not dare move while those silent, gold-caped birds flew through the air.

Suddenly a whoop filled the garden, a long, barbaric yowl that tore Patricia's attention from the trapeze artists. She saw a thick rope fall from the rear wall of the property and, climbing down it, Tarzan, in person, the same Tarzan of the matinées and comic books of her childhood, with his skimpy loincloth and live monkey on his hip. The King of the Jungle leapt gracefully to earth, thumped his chest with his fists, and repeated the visceral bellow, attracting all the servants, who rushed out to the terrace. With a wave of the hand, Patricia gestured to them to stay where they were, while the voice of Tarzan gave way to a lugubrious drum roll announcing a retinue of four Egyptian dancers who advanced as if trapped in a frieze, head and feet at right angles to their bodies; they were followed by a hunchback wearing a striped hooded cape and leading a black panther at the end of a chain. Then came two monks carrying a sarcophagus and, behind them, an angel with long golden locks and then, bringing up the rear, an Indian disguised as a Japanese wearing a dressing-gown and wooden clogs. All of them paused behind the swimming-pool. The monks deposited the coffin on the grass and, while the Egyptian maidens chanted softly in some dead tongue and the Angel and Kuramoto rippled their prodigious muscles, the lid of the sarcophagus swung open and a nightmarish creature emerged from inside. Once revealed, swathed in gauze, it was obvious that this was a mummy in perfect health. At this moment, Tarzan yodelled another cry and, with absolutely no provocation, began hopping around the Egyptians, brandishing the simian. The mummy lost its millenary patience, lifted one rigid arm and let it swing like a cudgel against the nape of the savage's neck, who fell to the ground, his face buried in the lawn. The monkey screamed and scrambled up a tree. Before the embalmed pharaoh could deliver a second blow, Tarzan leaped to his feet and fell upon the mummy with a roar. Locked in legendary combat, their rolling and thrashing freed the panther; the characters in the parade ran to hide in the garden and all the servants flew back to the safety of the kitchen. Patricia was about to jump into the pool when, as if by magic, an individual in tails and a top hat appeared and with one snap of his whip stopped the cat, who fell to the ground purring like a pussy-cat, with all four paws in the air; the hunchback recaptured the chain, as the ringmaster swept off his hat and pulled from it a meringue torte that he carried to the terrace and deposited at the feet of the lady of the house.

This was the signal for the remainder of the cast to march in from the rear of the garden: musicians playing military marches, clowns assaulting one another with slapsticks, dwarfs from medieval courts, an equestrienne standing on her mount, a bearded lady, dogs on bicycles, an ostrich costumed as Columbine and, finally, a team of boxers in satin trunks and boxing gloves pushing a wheeled platform crowned by a painted cardboard arch. And there, on the dais of a stage-set emperor, sat Horacio Fortunato, his mane slicked down with brilliantine, grinning his irrepressible gallant's grin, pompous beneath his triumphal dome, surrounded by his outrageous circus, acclaimed by the trumpets and cymbals of his own orchestra, the most conceited, most love-sick and most entertaining man in the world. Patricia laughed and walked forward to meet him.

Translated from the Spanish by Margaret Sayers Peden.

BILL ROORBACH
SUMMERS WITH JULIET

Hot Tin Roof

At eight I was interested in fishing, reading and the diligent
scavengering of fabulous pieces of glass and metal and,
sometimes, wood. I have clear memories of specific finds: a blue
glass insulator from a fallen telephone pole; a railroad spike from
the tracks behind Mike Didelot's; hundreds of thin, unidentified
strips of metal that I found on the streets of my lonely new home
town. I found coins and bike-pedals and spoons and, once, an
old cast-iron witch's pot. I even had a weathered board with
Chinese writing on it, which I'd found floated up at the beach on
Long Island Sound. How far had it come? (Well, probably from
Stamford or Norwalk or New York, but I had a grander vision).

At eight I knew about an old truck in the woods way back
behind our house, a Model A I thought, the lord of all treasures,
with speedometer and steering-wheel intact. I also knew about an
old steamer trunk which sat half-buried in leaves just off Jelliff
Mill Road. I had spied it from the height of the school bus, kept
it secret from all but Mike Didelot, convinced it was full of jewels
or some poor prince's head or a giant gladiator's outsized
armour. When Mike and I finally broke into the trunk, the
flowerpots were treasure enough, three of them, at least a little
bit ancient, and broken.

And when I was eight, unbeknownst to me, Juliet Karelsen
was born, 15 June 1962, away off in New York City, that tall
town where my father worked and where a penny could kill. By
the time Juliet herself had turned eight she was already an
independent little New York girl, owner of an elaborate doll's
house, maker of 200 faces, eater of ice cream, seller on the street
of homemade greeting cards, rogue child of Central Park West, in
charge of her parents, in love with her teacher, in cahoots with
the doormen, going steady with a black boy from school,
studying ethics, playing guitar, husbanding a hamster named
Willy. So sensitive, said a family friend, that she could feel the
grass grow under her feet. That summer, Juliet, bearing her
hamster, and in league with her little sister Eva, deigned to
accompany her parents to Wellfleet, Massachusetts, on Cape

Cod. I was sixteen by then, about to turn seventeen, and Juliet and I had kept our relative distance. New York City, New York, to New Canaan, Connecticut, is about forty-five miles. Wellfleet, Cape Cod, to Edgartown, Martha's Vineyard, is also about forty-five miles and in Edgartown I was on vacation with my own family.

I had to go to bird sanctuaries and museums and clothes stores and nature walks and church. We went to the beach in the mornings for a prescribed number of hours, then came home to the hotel for lunch. I babysat Janet while picking on Dougie and Carol, then in the afternoon was set free for three or four hours. I knew just where to go. In Edgartown you hung out on the lawn in front of the Old Whaling Church with cool kids from all over, kids who knew what it was all about. And on the Vineyard, when it wasn't all about how long your bleached hair was getting, it was all about James Taylor. There was always a party being rumoured and J.T. was always going to be at the party.

On the Cape, Juliet meanwhile would have been building a beach house for her doll family, a group made up of little European dolls Hans and Bridget: the parents; Susie, Debbie, Peter, David, Frank, Louisa and Christopher: the children; and Uncle Nick: their live-in dentist. Juliet and Eva and their friends sawed boards in the basement of her family's rented cottage until the dollhouse was done. There was no workbench in the basement, and no vices, just a saw and hammer and a pile of lumber; so Juliet made the other three hold on to the old boards, six skinny arms taut and trembling, as she sawed and hammered, intent on the work. When the other girls wanted to stop, Juliet said no. The doll family must have a beach house!

My seventeenth birthday came in the midst of vacation. As a treat I got to go out on my own; was given a midnight curfew. A wild luxury. Especially since I knew of a party at which not only James Taylor was guaranteed to show, but his brother Livingston too, and probably Carole King. The party of the summer. I dressed in my tightest black bluejeans and my hippest BVD undershirt (that brand had a *pocket*) and flipped my hair many times in front of the wavy hotel mirror.

The party was at an elegant old house, clapboard, square, white, the home once of a whaling captain, and now, having not changed hands all these 200 years, summer home of his progeny. Its door was painted red and was open. The music of Jimi Hendrix blared forth.

I gulped; gave my head a shake; marched up the steps of the austere porch. No one asked who I was. I accepted a mug full of wine, lit up a cigarette and found my way into the living-room and then to the hearth, where I could lean under the great mantelpiece and watch the proceedings. James Taylor did not yet seem to be in attendance. Indeed, no one older than eighteen seemed to be in attendance. I drank more wine; smoked another cigarette. I had a beer someone passed me; smoked a little pot. More wine. A drink of Jack Daniels. Some beer. Some wine. I never moved from my spot. On the mantel was an array of objects, all of which held real interest for me: an antique sextant. A large marine vertebra. An old, well-used bos'n's pipe. A real harpoon. A walrus tusk, scrimshawed. A baleen comb, made from the great plankton-screening maw of a sperm whale. Gradually I got drunk enough to forget the party and to pay attention to the treasures. A shark's jaw with triple rows of teeth. When had this shark swum? A little stone Buddha. How far had Captain Pendergast (that was the name engraved on a brass box) sailed? A pair of brass-and-leather binoculars. A glass float, round as the Earth and as blue, escaped from a fisherman's net in Portugal, I knew, but when? And around the room, photographs and paintings and etchings: grinning second mates, sheets of blubber, boats under full sail and adorned with flags and fresh paint and men in the rigging, leaving Edgartown harbour.

The Pendergasts also had a clock collection, thirty or forty old things, well kept and tocking. They all struck at midnight, a prolonged concatenation of bongs and dings and whistles and tweets. I stayed. Silly curfew! The party was going strong, doors closed, windows closed, music very low in fear of the ever-watchful Edgartown police. James Taylor on the stereo, as close as we would get to him that night. Someone had handed me a full jug of wine and I clutched it, staring up at a trio of rudely carved, life-sized, wooden geese. Full of wine, I spoke my first words of the night: 'I wonder what those geese were for?'

Soon a knot of us were sharing the wine and discussing the dustless birds. Too unmarked to have been used by any hunter as decoys. 'Too top heavy, anyway,' someone said, poking at one. 'Not weighted at all.' Each goose had a reddish glass eye, and feet painted on to its bottom. We argued. A young woman came up, the young woman who was throwing the party, a good forty or sixty pounds overweight, somewhat older than I, eyes brown and slightly occluded by her chubby cheeks as she smiled. 'They're boredom geese,' she said. 'My great-great-great-grandfather made 'em whenever he got stuck on land for too long.'

The clocks, all thirty or forty of them, struck one. Ms Pendergast, our hostess (her first name, I think, was Roberta), showed me a box of scrimshaw tools. And two narwhal tusks, the likes of which were once sold as unicorn horns. And a coconut-shell mask from Tahiti, made at the time Gauguin lived there. And a block of wood with leather straps, once some ancestor's replacement foot. The log of the frigate *Margaret*, dated 1807, which my hostess wasn't supposed to open, but did. Upstairs, Roberta showed me her bed, which had been the captain's bed on the good ship *Eleanor Alison*, *circa* 1830. Quickly, she got me out of her room as if her mother were about to catch us, and down the back stairs. In the kitchen were thirty more carved geese, a flight of them on two long shelves that met in the corner over the stove, 'A vee,' as she pointed out. 'Like a real flock.'

Downstairs, the party had dissipated to a few drunks and my tour guide's younger brothers. The latter were busy bouncing the former. The house was a mess. Soon, I noticed, everyone was gone but the two brothers, Ms Pendergast and I. My head was beginning to spin, the prelude to a night of vomiting in the shower while my father, disgusted, held me upright in the stall. 'Mom's going to kill us,' the youngest brother said.

'Who is this guy?' the other said, pointing at me with a back-flung thumb.

Spinning or not I lifted the big green jug of wine to my lips.

'My friend,' Roberta said. She certainly was fat, a good deal bigger than I.

'Well, Mom's going to kill us,' brother number one repeated, with special emphasis. The brothers were not fat, not at all.

I pressed on, undaunted. 'What's that thing?' I said, pointing.

'Blubber knife,' the bigger brother said, annoyed. 'Time to go.'

Ms Pendergast and her brothers walked me out on the porch. She shooed the boys inside and, apparently having mistaken my interest in her family artefacts for an interest in herself, she took my head in her hands and kissed me smack smack on the lips. Her hands on my head seemed to contain the spinning somewhat and her lips gave the whole fuzzy world a warm, wet focus. I put my arms around some of her, for support, and there we stood, lip to lip, till her brother came out and pulled her inside.

On the Cape, Juliet and her family must have been asleep after a night engaged in one of their ritual vacation activities. The Drive-in, Provincetown, the Dairy King, the Puritan Shop in Wellfleet. (On a recent camping trip she showed me everything: their various rented houses; the houses of her friends, Meyer, Winkelstein, DeCarlo, Waters; the Howard Johnson's her family always stopped at; the beaches they had most fun at; the place she bought her best bathing suit *ever*.) Juliet and Eva preferred the Buzzard's Bay side of the Cape where low tide made miles of flats to play on and everyone bragged of knowing someone who had walked to Provincetown across the sandbars before high tide came to drown him. The girls played marina, using shells as boats and digging channels which the tide would fill, rising. They stole *Once Is Never Enough* from their mother and read the sex scenes to each other as they lay under their towels in the sand. They brought Willy the hamster to the dunes so he could see the ocean and to Howard Johnson's so he wouldn't be lonely at home or too hot in the car.

My father at midnight was miffed. At one o'clock he was furious and worried, both, each emotion escalating the other. At two o'clock he went out looking for me. He got in the car (a wood-panelled station wagon) and crawled the streets of Edgartown with his lights off. Earlier he and Mom had taken note of a party at one of the old captain's houses, so he slunk over to that neighbourhood, and found me, sure enough, on the porch in the near dark kissing someone as big around as he was.

I went to Martha's Vineyard next in 1980 at the behest of my old college friend Jon Zeeman. I could afford the trip because I'd spotted a classified ad in the *New York Times* looking for someone to write a question-and-answer format home-repair book. (I got to New York four hours early for my appointment, stumbled through the interview, actually *fell* on my way out of the publisher's office, but got the job. Ten dollars a page for a 256-page book, 2,560 dollars, not much for a whole book, even at the time, but to me a fortune.) I told my then girlfriend Melanie I thought I'd try writing it on the Vineyard. Maybe by myself. She cried. I cried. Everybody cried, but I was determined to go and she was determined to let me.

When Jon came, I was ready. He had rented a U-Haul for his PA system and his amps and his Hammond organ. He meant to have a band and play for the summer tourists. We emptied my little house of everything I owned, which wasn't much, mostly odd bits of pipe and lumber and boxes of books, and headed for the Vineyard, Jon with his guitars up front in the car, me with my typewriter and my tools. In Oak Bluffs, fresh off the ferry, we took possession of 222 Circuit Avenue, a rickety old gingerbread cottage with six bedrooms, which would make room for the other two-thirds of Jon's jazz trio when they turned up and for two or three oddball room-mates to help pay the rent.

On sunny days our little household went to the beach. On the rare rainy days, Jon and his band rehearsed upstairs, thumping the floor. I typed in the basement, one or two frantic days a week, making the book. *Fix-It! Tips and Tricks for Home Repair.* Every fifty pages I'd send off to New York, then haunt the general delivery window at the Post Office until my cheque (500 dollars!) would arrive. I tried to make the questions sound like real people talking; used a lot of exclamation marks to show their excitement at the task ahead. *Q: My darn faucet is driving me crazy! How can I get it to stop dripping all night?* Or *Q: I'd like to build a bookshelf to keep this home repair book in. How do*

I go about it? or *Q: My son Johnny* [I always used my friend's names] *just had a snowball fight to end all snowball fights! How do you repair a broken window?*

At night, Jon's trio, The Circuit Avenue Band, played around the island, at bars, at restaurants, at parties. I went along and the four of us managed to meet a lot of women, which, after all, was the idea.

Juliet, being only eighteen, may or may not have been too young for our notice, though she was on Martha's Vineyard for a week that summer, visiting a college friend who was working as an up-island *au pair*. Jules was a freshman by then at the University of Michigan, had spent most of the summer working as a counsellor at a camp for disturbed kids, had had her own heart broken and learned what all those lyrics to all those James Taylor songs she liked to play on her guitar were really about.

The next summer, after an insolvent off-season in New York, Jon and the boys and I were back. Two summers later, we were back again. Jon and I found a cheap enough house near the sewage treatment plant on the outskirts of Edgartown, which only smelled when the wind came our way one night out of a week, or two. By now I was singing in Jon's summer band which had evolved into a jazz/rock/oldies/rhythm-and-blues/country band, somehow, and being paid half what the other musicians were paid. We hadn't enough money for restaurant meals, much less enough for a decent beach-towel or enough to fix our old bomb cars when they broke, but we had plenty of money for drinks at the bars, and plenty of money for admission to the Hot Tin Roof, which had been Carly Simon's place, a seventies-style disco in an old airplane hangar up in the scrub oak forest by the airport.

On the evening of 20 July I looked up from the bar there and spied a pretty young woman passing. She was blonde and flushed and had an aquiline nose (which word until recently I thought meant *straight*, but no, it means *like an eagle's*, hooked), and fairly glowed with aplomb. I kept my eye on her as she glided her way across the dance-floor and up the stairs through the crowd to the bar.

Jon came waltzing by, holding a beer. 'Have a look,' I said.

He peered brazenly back up into the balcony area, found the table in question. 'Blonde?' he said.

I pretended not to look. 'Right.'

'Nothing special.' And off he went.

I danced with friends nearer my age then—Sally from the Rare Duck, Messina from the beach, Ellie Winters from the book store—hoping to give the impression of my own popularity and insouciance. I drank beer. I danced. I went to the bathroom. When I came out, the blonde girl—Juliet—stood exactly in my way, having bypassed the line for the lady's room.

'Anyone in there?' she said.

'I'll check.'

She followed me in, scooted into a stall. 'Could you watch the door?'

I deliberated. Then, not wanting to seem too easy, I abandoned my post.

Later, when I found her near the dance-floor with her friends, she pretended not to know me.

'The men's room?' I said, to sharpen her memory.

'You!' she said. 'There was a crowd of pissing guys in there when I came out!' It seemed she found this funny. She accepted my invitation to dance. She told me she lived with her sister and a couple of friends in Vineyard Haven. She told me she was from New York. She told me she worked in a sandwich place, dipping ice cream. She told me she played guitar.

I told her my name, which on the Vineyard was Billy.

'Oh!' she said, with real feeling, 'I had a hamster once named Willy!'

Autumn comes early to the Vineyard. Leases expire on Labor Day. Flocks of geese start assembling for the flight south.

Juliet and I had formed a tenuous union which was about to be sundered by her trip back to Michigan. She seemed not the least troubled by that dark prospect. Late on one of our last nights, she decided we should sleep on the beach, away from the crowd of superannuated teenagers in my house and away from her basement apartment, where she and her three room-mates shared two small bedrooms equipped with but a double bed each.

Beach sleeping is not allowed on Martha's Vineyard. But we surreptitiously borrowed Joanna's car and headed to South Beach, where I was sure we'd be caught and arrested. Jules knew a place, a dirt road that ended high over a salt pond, near a darkened house. We took along all the blankets from her bed and one pillow and several beers, and tramped like sleep-walking children across the dunes and to the beach. We walked up-island a long way, past another couple who were already asleep. Finally we stopped, spread out our blankets and felt the cold wind and watched the surf coming in under the brilliant Milky Way, Venus coruscating near Mars at the horizon; enough light despite the new moon to illuminate the spray and the crests of the marching waves and to silhouette flock after flock of night geese arriving at the pond behind us. We shivered in our blankets, sipping beer, talking softly, kissing.

After a brief hour we saw flashlights coming. We held our breath, watching the couple down the beach get arrested and waiting, Juliet calmly, I pumping adrenalin. But the flashlight beams could not reach us and the cops turned back, satisfied with their catch. By five in the morning we had slept very little, had made sandy love and had decided to head back, to be warm in the car as the dawn arrived in pink and mist.

The pond, when we got there, was covered, acre after acre, with geese. There were thousands and new flocks arriving moment by moment: a busy airport. Juliet and I watched them from the windless warmth of the car for an hour. At sunrise the flocks began to depart, out over the ocean, big flocks then lesser ones, away in a chorus of honks from their fellows. I have never seen so many geese in one place; in fact, I have never seen so many of any single animal gathered in one place, except humans, perhaps, and bees. I thought of Captain Pendergast's geese, unliving on their shelves.

I'd always thought of geese as the end of things, flying off in melancholy V's. I grew sad sitting there on the big bench seat of Joanna's old car, overlooking the salt pond, which had become the very heart of endings, sitting away from tousled Juliet, my friend. Hard to separate endings from beginnings at times like that. Hard to think, oh, *time will tell*, as bright new Juliet waves from the ferry two days later. Gone. Hard to keep the melancholy out of the letters I wrote her nearly daily, some on birch-bark from New Hampshire (anything to impress), some on my brand new letter-head from New York (anything, anything). Hard to recognize the beginning of something, but there it was. And all those silly geese departing.

Fishing with Bobby

Juliet and I had wandered to Casey Key following an arrowhead camping symbol on our free tourist map of Florida. The month was March, we had finally found a warm part of the world, and best of all—after two days in our borrowed car—I was fishing for pinheads.

I used shrimp and 'bottom fished' them with a one-ounce lead weight. To bottom fish you tie the weight on a short length of light line so that it sits on the bottom while the shrimp floats a foot or so off the sand. I'd bought two dozen live shrimps that afternoon, but now they were dead: good bait for bottom fishing.

Juliet wandered the beach picking up trophies from the extraordinary concentration of shells on the high-tide line and taking pictures of the storm-clouds that sat just inland. It was probably raining where we had camped. I thought of our tent left open at the river and our sleeping-bags draped over the picnic table there and felt a tension which had nothing to do with Florida or wet sleeping-bags, but was left from New York. I cast again. We had tiny potatoes from an inland farm, a couple of big onions from Vidalia, Georgia, four ears of corn and a fire to cook on; we only needed a couple or three pinheads to have dinner.

Pinheads are small, less than a pound at the largest, six to eight inches long and built slim. They belong to the same family as porgies and resemble them: the same quill-sharp dorsal and anal spines, the same brutish profile, the same small mouth, tough and protruding lips, big eyes. Porgies are silver, however, and the pinheads were yellow.

Juliet snapped my picture. She was wearing my big red shirt over her new six-dollar, one-piece bathing-suit which was maybe meant to be a leotard, bought at a place called EVERYTHING SIX DOLLARS in Brunswick, Georgia. Her hair, I thought, was a touch blonder from all the sun we'd had during the afternoon. Her legs were certainly pink; my own face burned.

I got a bite, tried to set the hook, failed and reeled in a shrimpless rig. On the next shrimp I succeeded and my cheap new rod bent stiffly. Looking around for Jules I saw instead an enormous wing-span, double the span of the pelicans that cruised low across the water like bombers trying to avoid radar. A huge bird was flying straight at me, neck tucked in, which meant it was a heron and not a crane. I watched, kept reeling, absently. The heron hit the beach beside me, stumbled, pulled its wings in, looked embarrassed for a moment, then gazed steadfastly at the bend in my rod.

He was four feet tall, mostly legs and neck, and he kept exactly four feet away from me. He had big amber eyes which protruded from the sides of his slim head. He was pigeon-toed and had large unwebbed feet with three long toes pointing forward and a slightly shorter toe pointing backwards. So: herons were responsible for the perfect peace-sign footprints I'd seen in the sand at the bottom of an alligator pond in the State Park. He kept his wings tight to his body, hunched up at the shoulders. From his fuzzy head stuck a pair of plumes which lay flat when his head was in flying position in order to bridge the unaerodynamic gap formed by the S-curve of the tuck of his neck. As he stood on the beach watching my rod and pointedly waiting for me to reel in the fish, however, the plumes stuck out behind him like a poorly pomaded cowlick.

I pulled in the pinhead and, confident I'd catch more, I unhooked it and tossed it to the bird. My throwing gesture startled him and he stepped away, his body moving faster than his head could follow at the top of the long neck. The fish fell in the sand, flopping. The heron didn't care about the grit all over his meal; he snapped the fish up in his long hedge-clipper bill and again stepped away. Black-helmeted gulls began to gather as the heron grappled with the sandy fish. The heron tossed his head, tossed and clipped at the fish with his bill—not gracefully —tossed and clipped and juggled until the fish was positioned for a head-first ride down his throat. The heron pulled his neck in, then straightened it out, and the pinhead disappeared. The heron's neck distended just below his head in the exact shape of the fish. The heron shook his head and the fish moved downwards; the heron danced a little and the fish moved downwards; the heron pulled his neck in, shot it out, shook, wiggled, twisted, and the fish went down, its shape finally disappearing into the bird's football-sized body. I saw no evidence of peristalsis; it was gravity all the way.

The heron regarded me, waiting for more. He shook his head a couple of times, apparently pleased to have got the first fish down. I put another shrimp on the hook. The heron stepped closer, stood at my side as I cast. I let the weight sink to the bottom, forty feet out, and waited. The heron shifted his weight from foot to foot. I took a step towards him. He took a step away. I took a step back; he took a step towards me. He looked out to where my weight had splashed. He didn't want to dance. He wanted to eat fish. The sun had reached the horizon.

I pretended I had a bite by pulling back hard on the pole. The heron drooped his neck forward with interest, watched the rod tip intently. When I relaxed, he relaxed. After ten minutes he seemed bored, stepped away, walked along the water, had a drink. But each time I got a bite he trotted back. Juliet surprised us when she reappeared.

'Who's your friend?' she said. She took his picture. 'Put your arm around him.'

We showed her our dance. I got another fish on the line and reeled it in. 'Here's our dinner,' I said.

'Oh, give it to him.'

'I already gave him one.'

'Well, give him another one. I want to see him eat.'

'I want to eat.'

'There's more.'

She was right. I threw the fish. The heron, unconcerned for his image, ducked away, making no attempt to catch it in the air.

He was no golden retriever. He snapped it up quickly to save it from the gulls, went through his comic swallowing routine for Juliet and then eyed me, waiting for more.

I cast.

Two groups had begun to gather: laughing gulls and people.

'What sort of bird is that?' an older woman asked.

'It's a great blue heron,' I said.

'It's a pet,' Juliet said. 'Three years old.'

'What's its name?'

'Bobby,' Juliet said. 'He's like a son to us. Put your arm around him, I'll get a picture.'

I cast a new shrimp. Bobby was intent on my every move. More people gathered, stood at a safe distance from my casts, commented on the bird. I began to feel tense again. A young boy threw some sand. His sister shrieked. A youth said the bird was a crane.

'The fisherman said it's a heron,' the older lady said.

My heron stepped closer to me.

'You might as well split, Bobby my boy,' I said, quietly. 'The next fish is for me.'

He watched my rod, poised himself when it bent. I reeled in another little pinhead. I thought it would look nice delicately blackened on a paper plate with a roast onion and potatoes and corn. The heron leaned towards me. The kids grew silent. The older woman raised her camera.

'He's eaten too much,' I said. 'How many can he hold? He's got two pinheads in there already. Three's a crowd.'

Everyone watched, waiting, anyway.

'Go ahead,' Jules said.

I threw the bird the fish. I breathed, two-three-four, trying to relax. The heron shook my fish down his neck to applause and went to the water for a drink. He then stepped back to my side, closer yet.

'His pet,' the lady said, amazed.

I began to pack up my rod. The heron turned his head from side to side, assessing the situation. I bit the hook and weight off the line and tossed them at my tackle box. I put on my shirt, threw the shrimp out on to the beach. The gulls descended, roaring with laughter, but my heron tripped into the midst of them, snapping up shrimp. When he was finished he began to trot—five feet, ten feet, fifteen feet, fast, faster—stretched his wings, beat them and flew with big strokes, neck tucked back, suddenly graceful. He was full of fish and shrimp, and gone.

Callinectes Sapidus

On Martha's Vineyard there are two sorts of ponds. One is the normal sort: fresh water in a muddy-bottomed bowl, with bass and sunnies and a bench used by ice-skaters in the winter. The other is brackish, with tides, an outlet to the sea, occasional vicious bluefish and constant seagulls and terns, a sandy bottom and dune grass surrounding it. No matter how big these salt ponds get they are never called lakes. And though they have inlets to the sea, they contain too much fresh water to be called bays.

Some of the tidal ponds still have their original Wampanoag Indian names: Nashaquitsa, Sengekontacket, Squibnocket, Menensha, Paqua and Watcha; the others were named by settlers: Black Point, Chilmark, Edgartown Great, Tisbury Great, Jobs Neck and Homer. All were formed by sand bars turning into barrier beaches, closing off bodies of water. And all of the ponds serve as breeding grounds for shellfish and for bluefish, herring, mackerel and eels. And for blue crabs. We liked to eat the crabs.

With friends, Juliet and I had rented a big house at an exorbitant rate in the woods where we could worry about ticks and where we had a vegetable garden. To afford the house Juliet worked as a waitress and I used all my money and a credit card.

One of our room-mates, Louise, was tall and thin, with a taste for the heroic. One day she had the idea to go crabbing and grew very excited trying to enlist helpers. She said the way to do it is to tie a string to a piece of fish and wait until a crab takes an interest. Then you slide the bait towards you until the crab is in reach of your net, at which point—swoop!—you collect him.

'The creek at Scatter Neck is simply *full* of them!' This was typical Louise, all dramatic tones, talking very rapidly, trying to create some excitement. 'Blue crabs! They're *delicious*, they're *famous*! Who's got a string? Who would like to drive? You *guys*.' She'd done some crabbing in Maryland.

The first time they went, Juliet and Louise came home with eleven blue crabs, one of which was female and not blue at all. By Massachusetts law, one crab taken in ten may be female, so long as she is eggless. I stared at the crabs in their bucket. Their foreclaws were an incredible blue, the blue of the sky on the best day of summer, the blue of the water at evening, the blue of blue eyes, much brighter than the blue of blue blood, an artist's—Gauguin's—blue.

Eleven crabs for dinner! Louise was very proud—and Juliet too—as they explained how they'd captured the crabs; they laughed about all the splashing they'd done and laughed about the way the crabs seemed to run for your feet if you missed with the net. They told the story over and over as guests began to arrive. We boiled water and flung the poor crabs in.

The access to Scatter Neck is between the Tisbury Great Pond and Scatter Neck Pond. Tisbury Great Pond covers hundreds of acres. Scatter Neck Pond is smaller. Between them, behind the grassy dunes of the barrier beach, runs a tidal creek. The creek flows east to fill Scatter Neck Pond at rising tide, west to drain it at ebb. The current is never violent. Because the creek blocks easy access to the dunes and the beach and the sea, the Scatter Neck Association has built a little wooden foot-bridge to span it. I stood on the bridge and watched the water of the creek. It was clear. A crab shot past, heading east, zig-zagging in kicks and glides. Then another crab, heading west. They proceeded sideways, as crabs do, but swimming, which is peculiar to blue crabs and rare others. (*Callinectes*, in fact, is a nineteenth-century taxonomist's Greekism for 'beautiful swimmer'. *Sapidus* is the Latin for savoury, or tasty.)

From the bridge I could make out the bright cerulean blue of the male claws, the red and rusty orange of the female. We had invited no one to dinner. I envisioned us catching another dozen and having three to myself. Another crab flashed past. Another.

Tens of them, scores of them, east and west, hundreds, a highway, rush hour, none stopping, commuting between ponds.

'This is more than the last time,' Juliet said. 'Leave your sneakers on. They go for your feet if you miss!' She showed us a pink spot on her toe.

I put my sneakers on and waded in. On the bridge it had occurred to me that while Louise's technique was ingenious—she had smashed a mussel shell with a beer bottle, picked the meat out of the shell and tied it on a string, then dropped the mussel meat into the thoroughfare to tempt likely crabs into range—in the narrow creek there was no need for such cunning. The crabs rushed past. Tens, twenties, hundreds of crabs. I slashed at them with my net, laughing with my ineptitude. Ra, our household dog, stood on the bridge by our room-mate Lauren, cocked his head, raised his ears and adopted a stony silence.

I caught a crab.

'Female,' Juliet said, unimpressed, as always. 'They're slower, and you'd be too.'

Sure enough, there wasn't a spot of blue on my crab, and under the segmented flap of its abdomen was a dark glob of eggs. I turned the net over and the little crab fell gracefully back into the water.

Sunburned Juliet in her bathing-suit and sneakers joined me in the creek, which was growing muddy from all my thrashings. Lauren stayed up on the bridge, lying on her side like an Ingres odalisque in a stylish bikini, a languid look-out.

'Male!' she cried, and I charged with my net. 'Blue! Blue!' she exclaimed, and Juliet scooped up a female. 'It's a boy!' and I stumbled at the shadow rushing past, darted, lunged, missed and fell to my knees in the water.

After an hour we had three crabs. I thought dinner would be slight. The crabs rested in a joint-compound bucket, one of those big, white, five-gallon plastic buckets that will never deteriorate, ever, and that are useful for many things, especially crabbing. When you netted a good crab you flipped the net over the bucket, to turn the webbing inside out, then shook it and shook it to dislodge the crab, who hung on to the heavy mesh with his claws. You'd shake and shake until he'd let go with one claw,

then shake some more until he let go with the other. In the
bucket each new crab caused a ruckus.

A man wearing corduroy shorts and a polo shirt and a kind
of tennis-club hat—a floppy thing made of cotton with little steel
grummets to let the steam out—came up and looked at my
disreputable truck. Lauren and Juliet adjusted the bras of their
bathing-suits.

'Crabbing?' the man said. Next he would ask me for my
permit. 'You could use a better net.'

Lauren stood up on the bridge and explained Louise's
technique and how we'd given up on it, in the most pedagogical
tones. She rather defended my style, which I appreciated. I
demonstrated where appropriate. I even succeeded in catching a
good male and adding him to our cache with only seven or eight
flicks of the net. Ra welcomed the newcomer to the bucket.

'You might do better to stay still,' the man said. 'Let the
crabs come to you. You know the difference between a male and
a female, right?'

The question sounded proprietary to me; I bristled. 'The
males have the eggs?'

'We throw the blue ones back,' Juliet said. She lunged at a
speeding shadow in the water.

He seemed to agree that we were joking, and Lauren and he
discussed their Scatter Neck connections. They were both
progeny, it seemed. As Lauren and the fellow walked over the
dunes with Ra to the ocean, Juliet and I kept after the crabs,
perfecting our technique, needing suddenly to be extra-
competent.

The blue crabs were terrific dodgers, but, we learned, they
always dodged the same way. After a while we figured out which
way to swoop with the nets. The crabs came in waves, none for
five minutes, then scores. Some would see our feet and, having
escaped other crabbers, stop cold.

By the time the sun went down, we had twenty beautiful
male crabs. By the time Ra came back, we had twenty-five. By
the time Lauren got back with the man (who was named Robert),
we had thirty and were loath to quit, although we were wet and
cold and hungry and the sky was wine dark. Best of all, Lauren,

who was shy, had a date.

I put the bucket of crabs in the back of the pick-up, and Robert climbed in back there with Ra. Lauren and Juliet and I rode in front. Jules and I, well experienced at being brother or sister, said nothing, waiting for old Bob to get out before we began to tease. Not far from the gate Bob knocked on the window. I stopped. He leaped out. Ra leaped out. Lauren spoke. Ra leaped back in. We watched Robert walk to a house. Lauren admitted that she had made a date with him, and she was so serious about it that we didn't tease, but told her how nice we thought Bob was, and how tall and handsome.

At the corn pile that the Scatter Neck farmer made every evening we took some corn and left a dollar, then went home to make dinner. I boiled an enormous pot of water, which I tried to get the crabs into as humanely as possible. The crabs made it difficult; they held hands, as it were, creating an unbroken chain (just like that child's toy—I saw it at the dentist's office and again at my brother's house—a bucket of plastic monkeys whose hands hook together), impossible to drop into the water. I was able to lift the entire population of the bucket in a big knot, just by pulling on the first crab. Lauren called instructions. Our expert, Louise, was not yet home from work. I broke the chain with a couple of unmasterful shakes, which gave me six or seven crabs for the pot but added the problem of loose crabs on the kitchen floor.

Despite whatever compunction I might have had, the crabs—feisty and colourful as they may have been; eye-wiggling and claw-snapping and dog-scaring as they definitely were; under-the-dishwasher-scuttling and gorgeous and alive (I grant you this)—were items of food. I got them into the pot, using a thick leather glove and determination. Before long they were cooked, red as lobster and stacked up on the table and we were working them over and eating corn and laughing not to have guests.

Water

In Montana Juliet and I lived enamoured by water. Our cabin was a hundred yards from the river. The yard was full of wildflowers and ponderosa pine. The outhouse was hidden behind a cedar tree and there were no neighbours anywhere in sight, no sound whatsoever as dusk fell, no sound but the river.

The first morning I went to work trying to restore our landlord Theodore's water system. He'd explained it in hopeful terms but had mentioned that we ought to bring drinking water, just in case, and that the neighbour, Bob, had a manual pump on a deep, sweet well.

Theodore had a well, too, on the hill next to his old pick-up, but it looked to me as if it had been capped by the drillers. It may never have produced water at all. Heavy black polyvinyl-chloride tubing ran hidden in the high needle-and-thread grass from the hopeless well to the yard around the house and ended in the weeds. Another length of pipe led from the house almost to the river. A final piece with a wire-mesh, leaf-and-muck-encrusted cage on the end was meant, I thought, to be splashed into the river. Up at the cabin on further investigation, I noticed a nipple of white PVC pipe protruding from the outside wall above the kitchen area. I crept into the cabin, so as not to wake Jules, and climbed the crude ladder up into the loft where I discovered that the white PVC ran into an elevated fifty-five-gallon drum next to an eagle's-claw bathtub. A hose came out of the bottom of the drum. One branch led to the tub, the other downstairs and into the kitchen. It wasn't hard to figure out: stick a length of the black PVC into the river, connect it to the gasoline-powered pump Theodore had mentioned, connect the pump's outflow to the next length of PVC, stick that into the white nipple at the house, fill the drum, turn off the pump and presto: a fifty-five-gallon, gravity-fed cistern system.

I found the portable gasoline pump, also known as a ranch pump, where Theodore had said it would be, under a heap of flooring scraps and uninflated inner-tubes in the winter sun room, where the temperature was already ninety or so and rising.

Theodore had allowed that the impeller housing on the pump might be cracked, and perhaps he was correct, but I couldn't tell: the impeller housing was missing altogether. The carburettor, too, was missing, as was the spark-plug. A piece of stick had been threaded into the spark-plug socket. The pump, bless its heart (and Theodore's too), was little more than an iron weight, painted yellow.

I went fishing. The sun had just made the distant rocks at the headwaters of Paul Creek and glinted almost painfully from every wave crest. I felt the thigh-high current hurrying me as I stepped downstream in my hip-boots. The water, when I stuck my hand in, was not as cold as I suspected it might be. I cast a tiny nymph—a fly I'd tied in New York—into the current.

A mule deer was grazing her way along the crest of the rocky hill above me. Hawks were at work. Butterflies. Then bang and splash, a small trout was on my barbless hook, a wild brown trout, undamaged, spotted brilliantly in red and pink and shades of blue, a tough little fighter, anxious to live. I put him back educated and for ever wary (I hope) about the colour of brass in the shape of a hook. I kept wading, a quarter mile, studying mayflies and goldfinches and a possible bluebird, and fishing.

As I made the bend in the river I stopped. There was a deep green-and-blue pool ahead, placid under a sheer rock. Chipmunks made their warning—a distinct high *chip*—at my presence. Two small cabins were visible ahead. One would belong to Bob, the neighbour with the manual pump and the sweet, deep well.

The sun rose higher. The sky grew hot. If you think it is always cold in Montana, go and stand in that river when the sun is high. I stripped out of my vest and my shirt, tossed them to the rocks of the bank. Hotter yet. No more bites. I stepped to the shore and looked in the direction of the cabins and listened. Cicadas. Swallows. A bit of a breeze in the ponderosas. A pine-cone falling, branch to branch through its tree. Wing-beats of a lone duck. A humming-bird buzzing past, then two more. The river, of course, sloughing by in the deep. Nothing whatsoever else. I took off my hip-boots and my pants and my socks and dove in, floated downstream faster than I could walk, then swam hard against the flow in the deep water, thinking of the fish resting below me. At a full crawl I could just keep ahead of the current. When I relaxed, puffing, I shot downstream. The water was surprisingly warm, too warm for good trout.

Later I'd figure out that the river flowed across a treeless section of plains before re-entering the mountains. That sun-heated water passed our cabin twenty-four hours later. Twenty-four hours after a hot day the river would be warm. After a rainy day it would be cool. The current weather in our neighbourhood didn't matter; the river was a time machine. After two rainy days, its waters would be cold, the cold of the mountains, the headwaters, the melt-off of glaciers, the chill water of springs. After three days of rain, big trout from the Missouri would come upstream, following the precious chill.

I dressed and walked overland to our cabin, a little worried to be seen by some unknown neighbour. At home I found Juliet on the porch, drawing a bouquet she'd gathered of purple asters and butter 'n' eggs and columbine. Juliet is brilliant with pastels. She's slight and blonde and more serious in the morning than she is later in the day, when she grows boisterous and funny. She likes to be left alone as she works. In the house I was surprised to find that it was ten o'clock. Jules had a little pot of water on the stove, boiling it on a tidy gas flame which was fed by a tank of propane outside. I made the coffee for her and brought it out on the deck next to the sun room, a good way to get her to talk to me when she's painting.

She said, 'Did you get the water figured out?'

'Yes,' I said, 'It doesn't work.'

'It's beautiful here,' Juliet said. She drank her coffee. 'Now what about the water?'

The path to the river went straight from our door a hundred yards, then took a right and ran another two hundred yards along a rocky ledge above the river, then ducked to the water at a dead end formed by a twenty-foot-high cliff of old volcanic stone. I crouched on the flat jutting rock, hidden from the house, and pushed the big plastic vessel under. It blooped, filling.

As it filled, I watched the current. A log appeared upstream.

It floated towards me and stopped. It stared at me. It did not seem happy to see me. Its eyes were subtle, all brown, everything brown. The jug got full. The log stared at me just as long as it pleased, then quietly sank and disappeared. Later I figured out it was a beaver.

Water weighs about eight pounds per gallon. My plastic vessel therefore now weighed forty pounds. Forty pounds is a lot, in bare feet, even for a short walk. I made it up the steep path to the ledge, waddling with the unbalanced weight. Still several hundred yards to go. Forty pounds at the end of one arm gets uncomfortable quickly. I rested. I walked. I rested. Each stretch of walking was shorter than the last. My shoulder grew tired. My elbow felt disconnected. I pictured a cartoon arm, stretching. I made the last leg of the path in one speedy stumbling tack, hoping to impress Juliet, though we'd been together seven years and she wasn't likely to impress too easily. I *oomph*ed the water up on to the wooden deck, not far from her. Juliet looked at me briefly and went back to her painting.

I humped the water into the kitchen, poured two of the five gallons into a picnic jug that had a spout and the name BOB written on it in Magic Marker. Placed next to the sink, it would make a weak approximation of a faucet. I washed a glass Theodore had left there, using a sponge he had also left and some Dr Bronner's biodegradable dish soap, which Juliet and I had in our box of camping food and blackened pots. I pushed the button on the jug and the water flowed, rinsing the glass.

The evenings grew cooler. In Montana, autumn starts in August. Juliet mentioned hot baths more than they might normally come up in our conversation. I began to invent. The sun-room was a porch, really, nothing more than a deck with a Plexiglas roof and walls. Theodore had built it to have a warm bright place in the killing winters. By noon it must have been a hundred degrees in there. By two, 120. It smelled like the squirrels' nests it contained. I don't know why it took me three weeks to think of it, but I finally put our water vessel in there one morning after I had got myself in good enough shape to make the second trip to the river. I found that the top of a certain jar of Theodore's Folger's Crystals screwed nicely on to the spout of the vessel. I spent my fishing time drilling holes in the cap with a hand drill. I didn't say a word to Juliet.

In the chill just after a thunderstorm Juliet went out for a walk to collect wildflowers. I checked the water. It was not just luke-warm; it was hot, uncomfortably hot, nearly scalding. I poured some into the pot for the silverware, then added cold water from the BOB jug. I could barely contain my excitement. I wanted to surprise her, but when Juliet was back I could think of no way to trick her into taking off all her clothes and standing at the bottom of the stairs under the deck, which was just the proper seven feet above the pine-needle carpet below. I had to tell her. She stood naked and shivering, hugging herself, while I screwed the drilled Folger's cap on to our vessel, then sighed as I dumped hot river water over her head in a perfect shower. Two and a half gallons lasted only about two and a half minutes, but that was sufficient.

Juliet dried happily and dressed, grinning, as I stripped and shivered. Then she gave me my shower. I stood in the hot splash and pine needle puddle. I was proud of myself. Inordinately proud. We were clean, we were warm. Showers became a new daily ritual; the sound of splashing filled our yard; our ablutions grew complex: we poured water from the blue vessel into the steam pot and into the silverware pot to boil, then poured the boiled water back into the blue vessel. We added some cold water from the white vessel to make the temperature right, then Juliet got a shower as I emptied the blue vessel over her head. As she dried, I emptied the white vessel into the steam pot and into the silverware pot to boil, then poured the boiled water into the blue vessel . . . We spent hours at our water tasks, more and more absorbed by them as the days grew shorter and chillier.

We had a week of no rain at all and the river began to clear. On the morning of 18 August, which happened to be my birthday, number thirty-six, I climbed the hill next to the rocks that pointed towards heaven, climbed quickly, in good shape from water, climbed up a game path along brittle rock to the top. From there I could see the peaks of all of the small mountains we lived among. From there I could see the distant, high-mountain home of the headwaters of the river. I could almost see the Missouri, through our river's slotted canyon.

I looked down on our little cabin half hidden in the grove of ponderosas. Juliet was in there, still sleeping. I watched the river go by, saw the place to which it would go, saw many miles of its work, saw Bob's house and the ruined footbridge. I saw the place I lived; entire, uncomplicated, sublime, and thought, for one pixilated minute, that it was possible to live simply in the world.

A Letter for our Subscribers

Dear Subscriber,

At Granta, we do all we can to provide you with a fast, efficient postal delivery of your copies. Our service will be enhanced if you can remember these helpful points.

•Should you change your address, please tell us in good time. After each dispatch, hundreds of copies are returned to us because subscribers have moved without letting us know.

•If you have any questions about your subscription, please call 071 704 0470, or write to us at: Granta Subscriptions, 2-3 Hanover Yard, Noel Road, Islington, London N1 8BE.

•When you call or write, please quote your subscription number (you will find this on the top line of your mailing label), so that we can assist you as quickly as possible.

•Please use your postcode in all communications with us, as this can affect the speed with which you'll receive your copies and correspondence.

•We occasionally exchange our mailing list with other publications and companies if we believe their promotions may be of interest to you. If you would rather not receive any such literature, simply write and tell us, and your name will not be included.

Thank you for considering these few points. I hope you enjoy your new issue of Granta.

Yours sincerely,

Sarah Bristow

Sarah K. Bristow, Circulation Director

P.S. If you're not already a subscriber, isn't it about time you became one?

ROMESH
GUNESEKERA
A HOUSE
IN THE COUNTRY

The nights had always been noisy: frogs, drums, bottles, dogs barking at the moon. Then one evening there was silence. Ray stepped out on to the veranda. There was no wind. He pulled up a cane chair and sat down. The fireflies had disappeared. The trees and bushes in the small garden were still. Only the stars above moved, pulsing in the sky.

These were troubled times in Sri Lanka, people said, but nothing had happened in his neighbourhood. Nothing until this surprising silence. Even that, he thought, may not be new. He was becoming slow at noticing things.

Then a shadow moved. A young man appeared, his white sarong glowing in the moonlight.

He was much younger than Ray. Not as tall, but stronger, smoother skinned. His eyes were bright and hard like marbles. He came and stood by a pillar. A moth flew above him towards a wall light.

'What has happened?' Ray asked, looking around.

Siri scratched his head, gently rocking it. 'Don't know.'

'There's not a sound.' They spoke in slow Sinhala.

Ray liked this extraordinary silence. He liked the way their few words burst out and then hung in the air before melting. It was the silence of his winter England transplanted. The silence of windows and doors closed against the cold. Lately Colombo had become too noisy. He had never expected such peace would come so close to war.

'The radio?' Ray asked. Siri always had a radio on somewhere in the house, droning public service. 'Radio is not on?'

Siri shook his head. 'No batteries.' He bit the edge of his lower lip. 'I forgot to buy new ones. Shall I go now?'

It was late: nearly eleven at night. The little shop at the top of the road would have closed. Ray felt uneasy about Siri going too far. 'No. Go tomorrow. Better than now.'

Siri nodded. 'Too quiet. Maybe another curfew?'

But it was not simply the silence of curfew. There seemed to be no sound at all. In the two years Ray had been back in the country there had been many curfews. They had lost their significance. Only the occasional twenty-four-hour curfew had any impact. Even those rarely inconvenienced him; he was often content to stay in his house.

In recent months there had been a new wall to build, shutters to fix. Each day had been shattered by the hammer blows aimed at protecting his future privacy. Ray had taken to escaping to a bar in Duplex Road; it made him more than usually melancholic.

'Didn't you go out at all today?' Ray asked.

'These shutters,' Siri pointed inside. 'I wanted to finish the staining . . .'

'Good. They are very good.' The wood had the perfume of a boudoir.

'I was working on that, the last coat. Finished about seven-thirty. And then when I was listening after my bath, the radio stopped.' He twisted his fingers to show a collapse into chaos. 'I didn't go out then because I thought you would be coming home soon.' His face widened in an eager smile.

Ray looked away. His long shadow danced down the steps. A gecko twitched. Ray had come home late.

Siri shifted his weight and moved away from the wall. He sat on the edge of a step. 'What do you think they'll do, sir?'

'Who?'

'Government.'

Ray leaned back in his chair with both hands clasped behind his head and stared up at the night sky. He saw only a waning red moon. 'I don't know. What do you think?'

Siri rubbed his thighs. He'd heard people say they should hold elections—the government might even win; but people also said that there probably wouldn't be any elections. They'd try another 'military solution' against the JVP—the People's Liberation Front—like against the Tigers, and get stuck with war.

'Trouble is, no one knows.' Siri's mouth turned down at both ends, but his was not a face that could show much distress. 'Nobody really cares, do they? Except for themselves.'

Ray put his hands together, matching fingertips, and half nodded. 'Not many people do.'

R ay had not planned on having any help or company when he first returned to Colombo from England. He'd had a secure job with a building society, a flat in London, a car and a circle of acquaintances. There had also been a woman he'd spend a night or two with from time to time. But he never had much to talk about and quite often simply thought about going back to Sri Lanka. One summer she went back home to Ulster; she got married.

That year he too decided he would go back home.

He resigned from his job, sold his flat and left. The business of moving absorbed his energies and he had no time to think. He had a house left to him in Colombo and money saved over the years. He hoped he would find out what he wanted once he had freed himself from the constraints of his London life and once he had retrieved his past.

The first time he saw the house his uncle had left him, his blood turned to sand. It looked like a concrete box shoved into a hole. Nothing of the elegance of his converted London flat, nor the sensuality of the open tropical houses of his Sri Lankan childhood. But then he found Siri.

It was the luck of a moment. Ray was with a friend at a bar. They were drinking beer. His friend asked about the house and Ray said he had too much to do. He needed builders, renovators. His friend mentioned Sirisena, Siri, who had done their house.

A few days later Siri turned up. Ray liked his quiet competence; the strange innocence in his eyes. He didn't quite know how to develop their working relationship. To him it should have been simply a relationship of employment. The old roles of Colombo serfdom died years ago, but Siri kept saying 'sir' and circumscribing their roles. He developed his job from artisan, to supervisor, to cook, night-watchman and, in effect, the servant. Ray felt things had to change incrementally: he acquiesced and played the roles Siri expected. Siri himself was too deep in this world of manners to feel the pull of revolution being preached across the country.

Siri did the carpentry, found the plumbers, the electricians. He moved in and slowly rebuilt the old house around Ray. Walls were replastered, doors rehung, floors tiled. And he kept the house in order.

Although in England Ray had done many of these things himself, here he found he needed Siri. Much of the renovation was straightforward, but from time to time he would see the need for change. He would talk it over with Siri, his fingers designing in the air. The next day Siri would start on the work.

In this way a new veranda was created; rooms divided. The curfews allowed him to examine progress. They provided the snapshots when activity was suspended. The workmen didn't come; it was only Ray and Siri.

It was the first time since childhood that Ray had had a constant companion. He encouraged Siri to talk and wished, in a way, that Siri could turn into *his* confidant. He wanted to ask, 'Why do you treat me like a . . . ' but could never bring himself even to suggest he saw himself as a master.

Siri simply showed respect in his antiquated fashion.

Ray's only response was to care. He didn't know how to respect in turn, but he felt a need to protect in a way he had never felt before. He tried to be generous with the pay and reasonable in his demands, but Siri seemed to want to do everything that needed doing and to spend all his time in the house. He hardly ever went home to his village.

When Ray bought furniture for Siri's room, Siri looked dismayed.

'What's wrong?'

'I don't need all this.' Siri pointed at the cupboard and the new bed, the new pillow and mats.

'Some comfort won't harm.'

'I have nothing to put in the cupboard. The old bed was fine, just as it was.'

Ray said now that Siri had a steady job he might accumulate some possessions.

'What for? My family need things, my mother, my brother. I only need something to do. Some place . . . Sir, this house I am making for you. It will be beautiful. To me that is enough.'

Ray didn't know what to do. He was embarrassed and puzzled. He pulled down his chin and snorted, like a bull backing out of a shed. The early days were confusing. Siri was exhilarated by the freedom he had to use *any* material he desired to turn ideas into reality, even his own ideas. He had never been given such complete responsibility before. Ray didn't understand this. It took time for him to see Siri as himself.

That night, that silent night, back in his room Ray kept thinking about Siri. He felt uncomfortable. He would have liked to have talked some more. To have said something to Siri that would have helped them both understand what was happening. Instead they had sat there swallowing silence.

The next morning Ray woke to the scream of parrots circling the mango tree in the garden. He dressed quietly and stepped into the soft rubber of his shoes. In fifteen minutes he was out of the house.

The road was deserted. He walked to the end and crossed over into the park. He had a route he could follow with his eyes closed, carefully planned and timed to avoid other people. He liked walking alone, in control of the sound around him: the thud of his feet, the blood in his ears.

The sky that morning was grey. Large, heavy clouds rippled overhead. Crows crowded the flame tree by the main road. Bats hung on the telephone lines.

Usually Ray walked for about twenty minutes. On his way back he would collect a newspaper from the small general store near the temple. Then at home he would savour a pot of tea and read the news. This morning he was looking forward to returning to an almost completed veranda.

Siri would have prepared the tea and disappeared: a tray with a white cloth, a small blue Chinese teapot filled to the brim and protected by an embroidered tea-cosy, one plain white cup and saucer, a silver jug of boiled milk. Naturally also a silver spoon. Ray would normally find the tray on a glass table. He had learned to accept this service as a part of life. He no longer resisted it and he never did the same for Siri. He never went that far.

But sometimes, in the evening, he'd offer Siri a drink. He would find Siri sitting on the steps or stalking about the garden.

'Have a beer?' he'd say.

Siri would nod hesitantly and approach Ray, smoothing his sarong. He would take the glass and sip slowly. He never sat down when he had a beer. He would stand while Ray sat. Whether they shared a beer or not, Siri was usually quite happy to talk. He would tell Ray about life in the village: river bathing, family feuds, someone running amok. In the middle of such a story, Siri would sometimes stop and peer at Ray. 'Why do you look so sad?' he would ask and surprise Ray with his directness.

One evening Ray asked 'Have you built your own house?'

Siri's mouth wrinkled; he slowly shook his head. 'No. Not my own. I have no land.'

'What about the family farm?'

'It's very small. We have one field.'

His father had tried milch cows, but he couldn't compete with the local MP's people. They had commanded everything until the JVP moved in. By then the cows had dried up and Siri's father had died. His brother stayed to work the one field, but Siri left.

'Could you ever go back to live in the country again? Now, after a city life? After what you've learned?' Ray wanted to know how genuine his own feeling of returning to roots was. He knew it was never possible to go back to exactly the same things, but at the same time he felt the old world never quite passes away. Suddenly the frame shifts and you find yourself back where you started.

'Go back to the country? Village life?' Siri smiled like a little boy asked whether he liked mangoes. 'Yes. Yes, I could go back to a life in the country. Like my brother's. If there was a house like this in the country.'

'Maybe you should start saving some money?'

Siri found this suggestion amusing. 'There's never been the chance.' He clicked his tongue and added, 'Until now.'

The next day Ray went with Siri to the National Savings Bank and got him a savings book. He arranged for a part of his salary to go straight into savings. But even after that Ray felt Siri was still not thinking far enough ahead. He was going to lose out. It troubled him at the time, although his own concern about Siri puzzled him more.

Months later Ray heard that some private land was being sold close to Siri's village. He asked him about it.

'No, sir, I didn't know.'

Ray took a piece of paper from his pocket and unfolded it. 'Look; this is what it says.' He described the position of the land. It was near the coast.

'Yes,' Siri nodded. He knew the area.

'That land is a good price, I'm told.'

'I don't know, sir. But there's not much growing there.' He delicately licked his thumb and forefinger. 'You can taste the salt in the air there.'

'No, it is good land. You can grow cinnamon or cardamom. Something like that. I know Mr Wijesena has some land there.'

'Yes, you are right,' Siri nodded. 'He has grown some cloves I think. Are you thinking of buying some land also?'

Ray was standing by the door. He took a deep breath. Suddenly he realized he was nervous. Sweat ran down his back. Things were not very clear in his head. He had started talking about the land with the simple intention of planting a seed in Siri's mind: land was sometimes available. He had probably hoped, he now thought as he stood there, that Siri would connect the idea of his savings with the possibility of a piece of land out in the country. But as they talked he realized that it would take Siri years to get a living out of such land. That his life would be, at best, only a life of subsistence. He would sink into the earth, unless something radical could be done.

'I was thinking about a piece of land,' he said, looking down, away from Siri. 'I was thinking about you.'

'Me?'

'Maybe you should take some land?'

'Impossible, sir. Even with the savings you arranged. Good land in our area is expensive.'

'I know. But if you could, would you like some land? Is it what you want?'

'You know me, sir. I like to build. I like to grow. With some land there I can do both. And I can do as I please.'

'But when?'

'When my luck comes. When the gods take pity.'

'I can lend you the money,' Ray said quietly. It was not exactly what he wanted to say. The words slipped out like moonlight when the clouds move.

'But then I will be a debtor. I could never pay it back.'

Ray could see that. It could be the rut in the ground one never got out of. But he had a plan working itself out as he spoke.

'I'll buy the land. I'll *give* you a portion. You for your part can plant the trees for us both. Cinnamon or *cadju* or whatever.'

Siri's eyes brightened. There was a slight smile playing around his lips. The smooth boyish cheeks rippled. 'Why, sir? Why do you want to do this for me?'

Ray could say nothing except that he wanted to.

'You are very good, sir, very good.'

Ray made arrangements to buy the land and gave part of it to Siri, to the consternation of his solicitor. He felt better for it. He had followed his instincts. But his instincts had changed. They were not the financial instincts that had served him in London: land prices plummeted as the troubles in the country spread. But this did not worry him. Things had to improve, he thought. Meanwhile he was happy to be serving in his turn.

In about ten minutes he reached the top of the hill on the side of the park. His route had already curved so that he was in fact now on his way home. A few minutes' walk along the road would bring him to the shop where he collected his paper.

He noticed the sky was dark and smudged. The crows were flapping about. Down the road he could see the white dome of the temple near his shop. The flowers of the temple trees, frangipani, were out. White blossom. Those were the trees he would like to have on the borders of the land he bought for Siri. But the white of both the dome and the flowers was grubby, as though settled with ash.

Ray thought the sky should have cleared by now. He walked quickly towards the temple. By the wall he stopped to look again at the frangipani. Many of the white flowers had fallen. But in the garden next to the temple a tree with the blood-red variety of the flower stood in rich bloom. Ray was sweating.

Then, around the corner, he came to the shop: the charred remains of the shop. Bits were still smoking, thin wisps disappearing into the grey sky. A small crowd had gathered.

The vague thoughts in Ray's head evaporated; every muscle in his body was tense, but he felt extraordinarily calm. He stepped forward. 'How did this happen?'

Several people started talking. One man said the police had a statement from the JVP claiming responsibility. The shopkeeper was dead. He had been asleep inside. Kerosene had been used. Ray picked his way through the shattered glass and boiled sweets strewn along the roadside. Practically the whole of the tiny shop had been burned. One or two big blackened timbers still remained at the back, and buckled bits of corrugated tin from the roof lay like petrified sheets of magma. The old *na* tree that had shaded the shop-front was scorched; the trunk looked as if it had been gouged by a hot knife. Two policemen had cordoned off the place.

Ray waited for a while absorbing the babble around him, watching the smoke rise in small puffs out of the heaps of ash. There was nothing now to be done. The veins in his arms were swollen.

A store burns like so many others up and down the country. Only this one's closer to home. Nothing else has changed. But Ray knew that proximity made a difference. The air was pungent. He wondered whether the dust on his shoes now mixed earth with the ash of the shopkeeper's burnt flesh.

When he got home Siri was at the gate. 'Did you see. . . ?' Ray nodded and brushed past him.

Siri had heard about the fire from a neighbour. 'Is it very bad?'

'The whole shop has gone. Completely burnt out.'

'Mister Ibrahim?'

'Dead. He was inside.'

Ray went to his usual place. The tea-tray wasn't there. A fine layer of dust covered the table.

'Water's boiling, sir. I'll bring the tea now.'

In a few minutes Siri came with the tea. 'Will you have it

here on the veranda?'

'Inside may be better today.'

'You know, sir, they warned him. He was very foolish.'

Ray asked him who had warned the shopkeeper. Why?

'Several times they told him to stop selling those newspapers. Mister Ibrahim didn't listen. Even two days ago he told me that he will not stop selling newspapers just like that. But they said he must stop, or it will be the end for him. I don't know why he continued.'

Who had warned him?

'I don't know, sir. These thugs who come around.'

Ray raised his eyes. 'Why do you think he didn't stop selling those papers?' Ray asked. 'He was not a Party man.'

Siri shrugged. 'He was a *mudalali*. Making money. You make money by selling what people buy. People wanted his newspapers, so he sold them. That is his work. Was his work.'

Ray wondered if Siri was right. Was Ibrahim killed by the market? Or was he simply caught in between? He could see the flames leap at Ibrahim's straw mat; within seconds he must have been wrapped in fire. But he must have screamed. How did they not hear it? The shop was not far, and the night had been so silent. The smell of kerosene? Flesh? But then, countries have been in flames before and the world not known.

'Sir, do you think there is any danger here?'

'What do you mean?'

'Will they harm this house?'

'This house means nothing. It has nothing to do with anyone.'

'I hope no harm will come. It is becoming so beautiful.'

But Ray and Siri both felt uneasy all day. They avoided each other. Ray spent the morning alone and then went out to a café for lunch. He came back early in the evening and disappeared into his room. He had a shower and lay down on his bed to rest. Clean and cool; naked on the cotton sheet. He felt his body slowly relax. The evening was warm. As day began to turn to night the birds screamed again. Through his window he could see the sun set in an inflamed sky. When he closed his eyes the grey smudges came back. His skin was dry. He looked at the polished wood of his new windows. Siri had done a fine job. He had brought out the wood grain perfectly. Ray wanted to ask Siri to build another house. A house on *their* land out in the country. He thought if he provided the materials, Siri could design and build a house with two wings, or even two small houses. One for each of them. If Siri were to marry it would make for a good start. Ray wondered how he'd feel if that happened. He would lose something. The intimacy that had yet to be. But he would feel some satisfaction. He would have made a difference.

Later, when he came out on to the veranda he found Siri sitting on the steps. Siri looked up; his hard black eyes gave nothing to Ray.

'Sir,' Siri said in a low voice, 'I want to go.'

'Where?'

'Away, sir.' Siri remained sitting on the steps. His face was in shadow.

'What's wrong? What is it?'

'This destruction. I want to go away.' The eyes softened slightly. 'And you, sir, have seen the world. Tell me where. Where is a good place?'

Ray looked down at Siri. 'What do you mean? You know, shops have been burned many times before. In Matara, in Amparai, here in Colombo it has happened before.' But Siri shook his head. 'It has happened all over the world,' Ray said.

Siri kept shaking his head. 'But it can't always be like this. It can't.' The night air slowly curled around him.

'We have to learn. Somehow. We are no better, but we are no worse.' Ray turned on the wall lights, pushing at the darkness. Then he saw one of the new shutters was broken: several slats were splintered; the wood was raw. Ray felt a pain in his chest. He took a deep breath. 'Never mind. It can be fixed.' He was determined.

Siri stared at him, then shook his head again as if at a fly. 'Sir . . . ' his face slowly crumpled. 'Sir, my brother back home. They've used a lamp-post for him.' Siri shut his eyes.

Ray's throat felt thick, clogged. 'You should have told me,' he said at last, tugging at his neck. The body would have been mutilated, then strung up as a beacon; the corpse would swing in the wind for days. 'Why?'

Siri's bare feet dangled over the steps. When he spoke his voice was hardly audible. 'Who can tell, sir, in this place?'

Ray looked at their shadows cupped in a circle of yellow light on the gravel below the veranda; the light on Siri's arms. He tried to lean forward but couldn't move. He couldn't clear the space between them. Siri's skin was mottled.

'It happened last night,' Siri said.

Ray nodded, 'Maybe you should take a few days off. Find your people,' he heard himself say. 'The veranda can wait . . . ' His voice faltered. They were not the words he wanted. Ray saw himself alone again in his house, picking his way through the debris at the back. There were two rooms still to be done; the pots of yellow paint in the corner of the bedroom would remain unopened. He found himself thinking that without Siri he would have to make his own morning tea again. Drink alone on his incomplete veranda; wait.

But Siri said nothing. Ray could not tell whether he had heard him. Siri slowly straightened out and stepped down on to the path. He looked at Ray for a moment, then turned and started walking towards the back of the house, towards his room in the servant's quarters. Ray opened his mouth to say something about the new house, the cinnamon garden, but Siri had melted away in the darkness. Ray remained standing on the veranda. He felt he was on fire, but the palms of his hands were wet. Out in the garden fireflies made circles. Frogs croaked. The sky trembled like the skin of a drum.

MARTIN AMIS
TIME'S ARROW

I came rushing upward out of the blackest sleep to find myself surrounded by *doctors* . . . American doctors: I sensed their vigour, barely held in check, like the force of the growth of their hair; and the heavy touch of their heavy hands. Although my paralysis was pretty well total, I did find I could move my eyes. Availing themselves of my immobility, the doctors were, I sensed, discussing matters having to do with their copious free time. And the thought came to me, fully formed, fully settled: How I hate doctors. Any doctors. All doctors. Consider the Jewish joke, with the old lady running distractedly along the sea shore: *Help! My son the doctor is drowning!* Amusing, I suppose. But why the pride in these *doctor* children (why not shame, why not dread?): intimates of trauma and mortification, of bacillae and trichinae, the routine excruciations of *time*, with their disgusting furniture and their disgusting vocabulary (the blood-stained rubber bib, hanging on its hook)—life's gatekeepers.

The doctors around my bed were in leisurewear, a frieze of freckles and shorts, tan, arm hair. Insultingly casual though I found their manner, I was reassured by the very vapidity of these doctors or joggers or weight-lifters—something to do with their unsmiling pursuit of the good life. In my sleep I had dreamt . . . No: that sleep had been too dark for dreams. Presiding over that darkness, however, was a figure, a male shape, with an entirely unmanageable aura, containing such things as terror, beauty, love, filth and above all power. This male shape or essence seemed to be wearing a white coat (a medic's clean white smock). And black boots. And a certain kind of smile. I think the image might have been a ghost-negative of doctor number one—his black tracksuit and powerpack plimsolls, and the wince he gave as he pointed to my chest with a shake of his head.

Over the next few days and nights I moved in and out of consciousness. Great and unceasing struggle, with the bed like a trap or a pit, and the sense of starting out on a terrible journey, toward a terrible secret. The secret was of course inscrutable, but I knew it involved . . . it involved *the worst man in the worst place at the worst time.* I was becoming stronger. My heavybreathing doctors came and went (they didn't do a damn thing for me). There was a nurse, always, night or day. For some reason I kept shaking my head direly at her, whereupon she suggested that I go into hospital. Hospital? No way! She worked the drip (her uniform made a packety sound) and, annoyingly, kept taking my pulse and peering under my eyelids; I stuck my tongue out at her and she checked on that too. Because I was feeling much better now, really tiptop. Sensation and all its luxuries returned first to my left side (suddenly) and then to my right (with exquisite stealth). Deploying my new-found litheness, I could almost turn over in bed—more or less unassisted! I lay there gurgling proudly to myself for however long it was, as time went on by like this in hilarious futility, until the big day: the nurse disconnected me, and packed up her stuff and left; two golfing doctors backed themselves solemnly into the room and attended to me with climbing agitation; and then—if you don't mind—two young orderlies hurried in, roughly clothed me, and stretchered me out into the garden! Then I must have blacked out.

And when I came to it was with an audible pop in the ears, and a rich consciousness of solitude, and a feeling of love and admiration for this big stolid body I was in, which even now was busy and unconcerned, straining out over the rose bed to straighten an errant swathe of clematis on the wooden wall. The big body worked on, with slow competence—yes, it really knows its stuff. I kept wanting to take a good look at the garden but something isn't quite working—this body I'm in won't take orders from this mind of mine—and I had to make do with peripheral vision: the swooping and trembling flora, like pulses or soft explosions in the side of the head. And a circumambient pale green, barred and embossed with pale light, like . . . like American money. I worked on out there until it began to get dark. Is it dusk coming? Or is it dawn? I put the tools in the hut. Wait a minute. Why am I walking *backward* into the house? What is the—what is the sequence of this journey I'm on? What are its rules? Why are the birds singing so strangely? Where am I heading?

A routine, in any event, has certainly established itself. It seems I'm getting the hang of things.

I live, out here, in washing-line and mailbox America, innocuous America, in affable, melting-pot, primary-colour, You're-OK-I'm-OK *America*. My name, of course, is Tod

Friendly. Tod *G.* Friendly. Oh I'm there, I'm there at the produce store, at the Post Office, with my 'Hi' and my 'Bye now', my 'How are you?' and my 'Good. Good.' But it doesn't quite go like that. It goes like this:

'Dug. Dug,' says the old guy in the car-park.

'Dug,' I join in. 'Dug. Oo yah owh?'

'Aid ut oo yah owh?'

And then I walk away, backwards, with a touch of the hat. I speak without will or volition, in the same way that I do everything else. My head translates it, out of interest. There's a third language in here too: hiding. I sometimes dream in it.

But, yes, silver-haired, thick-skinned, with the *Gazette* under my arm, past the little driveways (THICKLY SETTLED), the lettered mailboxes (Trilling, Cohen, Meleagrou, Rezika, Bzinski and I don't know what-all), the quiet ambition of every homestead (Please Respect Owner's Rights), the child-filled squares of green and the yellow sign saying SLOW—CHILDREN and the silhouette of that precipitate youngster with his schoolbag, tearing, tearing. When the kids squeeze by me in the supermarket I give their mops the chaste old tousle. Tod Friendly. Each pair of eyes, even as they narrow in ingenuous greeting, draws a bead on something inside me, and I feel the heat of fear and shame. Is that what I'm heading toward? This fear, when I stop and think about it, has to do with my own mutilation. (I can't explain.) Who will commit it? How can I avert it?

Because I'm getting younger. I am. I'm getting stronger. I'm even getting *taller*. My mind follows this body around. Everything is familiar but not at all reassuring. Far from it. All the other people are getting younger too. They don't see the oddity of it. They don't find it faintly disgusting, as I do. I'm the only one who really notices. The others, they're not important in this. It's all for me, and I watch like the first-person onlooker in my own dream. They're lucky. I bet they don't have the dream I have. The figure in the white coat and the black boots. In his wake, a blizzard of wind and sleet, like a storm of human souls.

I mean, is it just me, or is this some kind of weird existence? All life, for instance, all sustenance, all meaning (and a good deal of money) issues from a single household appliance: the toilet handle.

At the end of the day, before my coffee, in I go. I lower my pants and make with the magic handle. And there it is: the humiliating *warm* smell. The toilet paper comes up into your fingers, you clean it on your rear end and then deftly wind it back on to the roll. The other transaction occurs. You pull up your pants and wait for the pain to go away. The pain, perhaps, of the whole transaction, the whole dependency. Glance down at the clear water in the bowl. I don't know, but it seems to me like a hell of a way to live. Then the two cups of decaff before you hit the sack.

Eating is a drag too. First I stack the clean plates into the 'dishwasher', which works OK, I guess, like all my other appliances, except when some fat bastard shows up in his jumpsuit and traumatizes them with his tools. All right: then you take a soiled dish from the machine, collect some scraps from the garbage can, and settle down for a short wait. Various materials are gulped up into my mouth, and after I've massaged them into shape with tongue and teeth I transfer them on to the plate and sculpt them up with knife and fork. That bit's quite soothing at least, unless you're eating soup or something. Next you get the laborious business of cooling, of reassembly, of storage, before their return to the store, where, admittedly, I am promptly and generously reimbursed for my trouble.

Another thing that really disappoints me about this life I'm living through: the reading. Of course I have no choice about any of my activities, and that I can more or less accept. But the reading! I get out of bed each night to start the day—and with what? Two or three hours of the *National Enquirer*. I begin at the bottom of the column and fight my way up the page to find each story summarized in inch-high type. MAN GIVES BIRTH TO DOG. Or GIRL RAPED BY MOTHER'S GHOST. Merle Oberon is reborn as a cat. All this stuff about *twins*. A Nordic super race will shortly descend from the cosmic iceclouds. All this stuff about *Atlantis*. Appropriately, it is the garbage people who bring me my reading matter. I bring in the bags—which issue, it would seem, from the monstrous jaws, the industrial violence, of the garbage truck. And so I sit here drooling into my glass and soaking up all that moronic dreck. The eyes of Tod Friendly, they sometimes wander, as he moves solidly around the room. The dusty bookcase; beyond its glass, the dusty spines of books all standing to attention. *The Sorrows of Young Werther. The Philosophy of Right*. But no. MY FATHER MARRIED A PIG. I AM GRETA GARBO SAYS MONKEY. SIAMESE QUINS!

There are certain pluses now, though, as the years lurch past, at their chosen stop-start rhythm. Physically I'm in good shape: never better. My ankles and spine and neck no longer hurt when I get out of bed. All of a sudden my bearing is superb. My hair is getting thicker, even though my visits to the barber are no more frequent than before: I trudge along there every couple of months. I'm feeling so great that I've even taken up tennis. Perhaps prematurely. Because—to begin with, at least—it made my knees hurt like a bastard. It's a pretty dumb game, I'm finding: you go out there, all sweaty from the shower; the ball jumps out of the net, or from the chicken wire at the back of the court, and we bat it around for a while until it is arbitrarily pocketed by the server. Yet we leap and snort away, happily enough. All the matches finish dead even. *Pap* say the rackets. The four of us josh and kid: our trusses, our elbow supports. The guys seem to like me. Why do I hate them for it? Why do I think they are fools, dupes? I can feel Tod Friendly's glands burning with some unguessable mixture of envy and contempt . . . Now, in the supermarket, the eyes of Tod Friendly linger on the bodies of the local frauleins as they pull their carts. I have long been hoping that Tod's eyes would start doing this. The calves, the join of the hips, the inlet of the clavicle, the eyes. It turns out, too, that Tod has a blue tin with photographs of women in it. Gay old broads in party dresses and tan pants suits. Letters, lockets, the remnants of love. Further down in the chest, where Tod doesn't often burrow, the women get quite a lot better-looking and start to wear things like swim-suits. If this means what I think it means, then I'm impatient. I really can't wait. I don't know how much sense it makes to say that I am tiring of Tod Friendly's company. We are in this together, absolutely. But of course he doesn't know I'm here. *His* isolation is complete; and it is left for me to sense the inordinate heaviness of his every thought and feeling. So each night we stagger to our feet and pick our clothes off the floor, and then sit and drool into our glass, staring at the tabloid and all its gruesome crap.

I can't tell—and I need to know—whether Tod Friendly is kind. He takes toys from children, on the street. He does. The kid will be standing there, with flustered mother, with big dad. Tod'll come on up. The toy, the squeaky duck or whatever, will be offered to him by the smiling child. Tod takes it. And backs away with a grin. The child's face turns blank. Both toy and smile are gone: he takes both toy and smile. Then he heads for the store, to cash it in. For what? A couple of bucks. Can you believe this guy? If there's fifty cents in it, he'll take candy from a baby. Tod goes to church and everything. He plods along there on a Sunday, in hat, tie, dark suit. The forgiving look you get from everybody on the way in—Tod seems to need it, the social reassurance. But it's clear what he's after. Christ, he's so transparent. He always takes a really big bill from the bowl.

It's strange to me. I know I live on a fierce and magical planet, which weeps or sweats rain or even flings it off in whipstroke after whipstroke, which fires off bolts of electric gold into the heavens at 186,000 miles per second, which with a single shrug of its tectonic plates can erect a city in half an hour. Creation . . . is easy, is quick. There's also a universe, apparently. But I cannot see the stars even though I know them to be there, because Tod sees them and at night is always cooing upward like everybody else, and pointing. The Plough. Sirius, the dog. I wonder why I can't see them, why the stars just aren't there for me. Maybe—for me—light is travelling the other way and my eyes will take a million years to find them in the night. Of the stars, two alone I see. The sun. And the planet they call the evening star, the morning star. Intense Venus.

There are love letters—I know it—in that blue tin of Tod's. I tell myself to be patient. Meanwhile, sometimes, I fold up and seal and send off letters I haven't written. Tod makes them, with fire, over in the grate there. Later we stroll out and pop them in the mailbox. They are letters to me, to us. For now, there's just this one correspondent: the same initials at the foot of the page. The letters seem very bland to me. Repetitive, too. They offer vague reassurance, in the vaguest terms. But Tod has a different take on them. All night his physiology speaks of alerted fear, of ignoble relief.

These developments all came one after the other. Things have really been buzzing around here. A new home. A career. The use of an automobile. And a love life.

The move was a perfectly symmetrical operation: lucid, elegant. Big men came, and loaded all my stuff on to their pick-up. I rode with them (we tossed the one-liners back and forth) to our destination. Which was the city. South of the dividing river, over the tracks, beyond the stockyards and their rusty corsetry, their arthritic cranes. The actual property is smaller than what we're used to; it's in a low row of terraced cottages, with a little back yard. I'm delighted with the new place because there are people everywhere here, but Tod is definitely in two minds about it. I can tell. For instance, just before we moved, while the men were still lurching around with their crates and cardboard boxes, Tod slipped out into the garden; he lowered himself to his knees, and, sniffing hungrily, richly . . . It was weird. Dewlike drops of moisture formed on the dry grass—and then rose upward through the air as if powered by the jolts in our chest. The moisture bathed our cheeks, deliciously, until with our tickling eyes we drank it in. Such distress. Why? I assume he was crying for the garden and what we'd done to it, over the years. The garden was heaven when we started out, but over the years, well, don't blame me is all I'm saying. It wasn't my decision. It never is. So Tod's tears were tears of remorse. At what he'd done. Look at it. A nightmare of wilt and mildew, of fungus and blackspot. All the roses and tulips he patiently drained and crushed, then sealed their exhumed corpses and took them in the paper bag to the store for money. All the weeds and nettles he screwed into the soil (and the earth took this ugliness, snatched at it with a sudden grip). Such, then, are the fruits of Tod's meticulous vandalism. Greenfly, whitefly, sawfly are his familiars. And horsefly. He seems to summon them to his face with a slow flick of the wrist. The muscle-bound horseflies retreat and return; they rest, rubbing their hands together in anticipation and spite. Destruction—is difficult. Destruction is slow.

Creation, as I said, is no trouble at all. Like with the car. One of the first things we do, after settling in—we show up at this raggedy little garage cum breakers' yard, about eight blocks south, past the gap-toothed projects, the flattened warehouses. Tod certainly gets my respect for the way he seems to know his way around. I'd call this garage a hole-in-the-wall operation—but there's no wall to hack a hole in. The buildings are right down on their knees. That's evidently the thing with the contemporary city. No one is seriously expected to live or work in it. Content, meaning and content, are all stored uptown, in the notched pillars of the skyscrapers. Well, the car looked OK. It looked like any other car. But Tod just stood there shaking his head at it. The garage guy stood beside him, wiping an oily rag with his oily fingers. Next, Tod goes and gives him 800 bucks. After that they argue for a while, Tod saying 900, the guy saying seven, then the guy saying six while Tod holds out for a thou. Left alone, Tod contemplated the car doubtfully; he ran his fingers along the bodywork. Searching for what, I didn't know. Scar tissue. Trauma . . . Every day we returned; and every day that car of ours was in sorrier shape. Eight hundred dollars! And you could actually see them at it, the grease monkeys, with their hammers and spanners, about their long chore of patient wreckage.

Needless to say, by the time we went along to 'claim' it (elsewhere: uptown), Tod's car was a total heap. The transaction also included a most unwelcome preliminary. Hospital. Yeah: a look-in at Casualty. We made our own way there. Somehow Tod knows this town backward. And we didn't stay long, thank God. We answered the questions put to us by the smocked orderly; we took off our shirt and got prodded and tapped. We kept our head down and barely sensed the strangled roar of indecipherable confusion, shame, pain, humourless atrocity. I tell you, hospital is some scene. I knew that. Always I knew it. The paramedic drove me uptown to the scene of the accident. My car, as I said, was a ruin, and I didn't feel too great myself as the police officer helped wedge me into its driving-seat and attempted to shut the warped front door. Thereafter I sat back and let Tod handle everything. There were all kinds of people staring in at us, and Tod himself seemed a little fazed at first. But then he got on with it. He rammed his foot down on the brake, and sent the car into a fizzing convulsion of rev and whinny. With a skilful lurch he gave the bent hydrant on the sidewalk a crunchy shouldercheck—and we were off, weaving at speed back up the street. Other cars squealed in to fill the sudden vacuum of our wake.

Minutes later: the first whispers of a love life. The idlest coincidence, I assume. We came home, Tod flooring the accelerator to bring about a violent halt. He hurried inside, obviously still pretty shaken up, and made a snatch for the phone. After the dialling tone there was a long silence before a woman's voice said, 'Durtsab!' I tried to concentrate. I think I got most of it. It went like this.

'So tell,' he said 'Tell who? God?'

'I'm going to tell on you.'

'Irene.' (That's her name.)

'I know you're evil,' she said. 'I know you're the worst man.'

'You don't know my secret,' he said. 'You just know I have one.'

'I knew it the way you made love.'

'Oh yes?'

'You say it in the night. In your sleep.'

'Oh yes?'

'I know your secret.'

'What is it?'

'I want you to know something.'

'Irene, you're drunk,' he said, and sighed.

'Hello there, lover man.'

Then Tod hung up on her. He put the phone down and listened to its ringing—its machine warble. His feeling tone was blank, was clear. But the sound spoke to me of exhaustive disenchantment—absolute and mutual—as if love and sex were there, but all used up, and used up long ago. It's funny. Tod was nervous before the call. I was nervous after it was over. Love in some form or other is approaching nearer. I hope it's all going to come natural. Of course I'm nervous. This will be my first time, after all. I hope it will be with someone I love.

I wished Tod would go and dig out that blue tin of his, so I could get a proper look at this Irene. But he didn't, of course. Fine chance.

Maybe love will be like driving.

'Pop? Your driving days are over.' So said the mechanic in his oily dungarees. So said the hospital orderly in his cool white smock. But they were wrong. On the contrary, our driving days have just begun. I think Tod must be hankering for the old house, over to Wellport, because that's where most of our trips end up. He's kept a key. We go in and look it over. It's empty now. He sizes things up. He appraises things. It's done with love, this measuring. More recently we've started looking at other properties in the general neighbourhood. But none of them is worth measuring, like our old place. The people in the other houses are extremely pleased to see us, but Tod just looks right through them.

We've started finding love letters in the trash, letters from Irene. Maybe love will be like driving. When people move—when they travel—they look where they've come from, not where they're going. Is this what the humans always do? Then love will be like driving, which doesn't appear to make much immediate sense. I mean, you have five reverse gears and only one for forward, which is marked 'R', for Reverse. When we drive, we don't look where we're going. We look where we came from. There are accidents, sure, and yet it all works out. The city streams and pours in this symphony of trust.

My career . . . I don't want to talk about it. You don't want to hear about it. One night I got out of bed and drove—very badly—to an office. I then had a party with my new colleagues. At six o'clock I went to the room with my name on the desk, donned a white coat, and started work. What at? Doctoring!

Tod's dreams are full of figures who scatter in the wind like leaves, full of souls who form constellations like the stars I can't see. He is conducting a long argument, and he is telling the truth, but the invisible people who might hear and judge luckily refuse to believe him and turn away with infinite weariness and disgust. Sometimes he is stoically mutilated by painfully fat burgers and aldermen. Sometimes he glows with great power, power lent by the tutelary maker who presides over all his sleep.

He is travelling toward his secret. Passenger or parasite, I am travelling there with him. It will be bad. It will be bad, and not intelligible. But I will know one thing about it (and the certainty is comforting): I *will* know *how* bad the secret is. Already I know this. I know that it is to do with shit and trash, and that it is wrong in time.

A s life speeds up like this I move among the urban people, in the urban setting, the city's metal and mortar, its sharper interactions, with more grit and bite in its gears. The city—and there are bigger cities than this—does things to the people who live in it. Does most things, perhaps, to the people who shouldn't *be* in the city. Tod Friendly, I think, shouldn't be in the city. Oh, he quite likes it, in some ways; he's stopped driving out to Wellport but I bet he misses our time there, its vigourlessness so safe and morally neutral, when he wore the venerable uniform of old age. (The old aren't cruel, are they. We don't look to the old, to the stooped, for cruelty. Cruelty, which is bright-eyed, which is pink-tongued.) Together with Tod's growing vigour I sense also a growing unease. I have no access to his secret. His secret moans down there in Tod's gut. I have no access to his thoughts. And what would his thoughts say, anyhow? I get the impression that *sequentiality*, for instance, is not a big thing with people's thoughts. These thoughts would swoop and jabber, coming from all directions. Like faces with mean little mouths. With mean little teeth.

This is more than city. This is inner city. And despite his new-found professional status, Tod lives among the *underclass*. Under, inner—how does the condition express itself? . . . Jesus, how do cities get here? One can just about imagine the monstrous labours of the eventual demolition (centuries away, long after my time), and the eventual creation of the pleasant land—the green, the promised. But I'm awfully glad I wasn't around for the city's arrival. It must have just lurched into life. It must have just lurched into life out of a great trodden stillness of dust and damp. My colleagues at Associated Medical Services, they tend to live, prudently and intelligibly enough, up on the Hill or in the western suburbs, toward the ocean. But perhaps Tod Friendly has need of the city, where he can always move among others, where he is never considered singly.

As for my career move, it began like so. One night about a month ago, I woke up in unusually poor shape, half clothed, in fact, and with the bedroom intolerably slewing around me as if tethered to a loosening capstan inside my chest. I got out of bed and put the rest of my clothes on. Jesus: no wonder I felt so awful yesterday (for yesterdays are always awful, when Tod really hits the tea). Then we did a weird thing. It felt 'significant': coyly significant. We went into the living-room and seized the brass clock which has for so long adorned the shelf above our fireplace, and violently enclosed it in the wrapping-paper and ribbons that we found in the trash. Tod stood there for a moment, staring at the mirror with a grin of contempt. The room was still reeling. Counter-clockwise. In the car we shimmied our way to the welcoming party at Associated Medical Services, on Route 9. Tod, incidentally, unloaded the clock on one of the nurses, little Maureen, a fair and freckly type whose large amorphous mouth seemed designed to express only powerlessness. Powerlessness: hope and no-hope, both at the same time.

Well, I can't claim that this doctoring business came as a total surprise. For a while now the narrow house has been filling up with medical paraphernalia, with doctoring tackle. Books about anatomy, born from fire in the back yard. Prescription pads. A plastic skull. One day Tod took from the trash a little framed certificate and went and hung it on the nail in the toilet door. With amusement he surveyed it—for several minutes. And of course I'm delighted when something like this happens, because words make plain sense, even though Tod always reads them backward. Some snippets from the certificate:

> I swear by Apollo Physician, by Health, by Panacea, and by all the gods and goddesses, making them my witnesses, that I will carry out, according to my ability and judgement, this oath and this indenture . . . I will keep pure and holy both my life and my art. In whatsoever houses I enter, I will enter to help the sick, and I will abstain from all intentional wrongdoing and harm . . .

Tod had a good laugh at that, as well he might . . . Also, the characteristic black bag, swung out of a closet. Inside, a world of pain.

The actual doctoring I'm pretty stoical about. Not that I have any say in the matter. I don't give the orders around here; really, I'm just along for the ride. So stoicism, I figure, is my best option. Tod and I seem to be on top of the work, and nobody complains. Up until now we've been spared any of the gorier stuff they do here—and some of this stuff you just wouldn't believe. Surprisingly, Tod is known and mocked and otherwise celebrated for his squeamishness. I say *surprisingly* because I know Tod *isn't* squeamish. *I'm* squeamish. I'm the squeamish one. Oh, Tod can hack it OK. His feeling tone—aweless, distant, scornful—is quite secure against the daily round in here: the routine mortifications, the constant sense of anxiety and tenderness poised against a puerile *esprit de corps*, the sounds of grief, the stares of vigil, and the smell of altered human flesh. Tod can take all this—whereas I'm harrowed by it. For me, work is an eight-hour panic attack. I'm trying hard to understand the question of violence, to understand that violence is necessary, salutary, that violence is good. But I can find nothing in me that assents to its ugliness. I was always this way, I realize, even back in Wellport. A child's weeping calmed by the firm slap of the father's hand, a dead ant revived by the indifferent press of a passing sole, a wounded finger healed and sealed by the knife's blade: anything of that kind made me flinch and gag. Christ, I couldn't see an aspirin without wanting to throw up. But the body I live and move in, Tod's body, feels nothing.

We seem to specialize in the following things: paperwork, gerontology, maladies related to the central nervous system, and what they call *talkdown*. I sit there in my white coat, with my reflex hammer, tuning forks, small flashlight, tongue blades, pins, needles. My patients are even older than I am. It has to be said that they usually look pretty cheerful on their way in. They turn, and sit, and nod bravely. 'Good,' says Tod. The old party then says, 'Thank you, doctor,' and hands over his prescription. Tod takes the scrap of paper and does his little stunt with the pen and pad.

'I'm going to give you something,' says Tod, 'that will make you feel better.' Which is pure bull, I know: any moment now, Tod's going to stick his finger up the poor guy's ass.

'Scared,' says the patient, undoing his pants.

'You seem fine to me,' says Tod. 'For your age. Do you feel depressed?'

After the business on the couch (a rotten deal for both of us: how we all whimper), Tod'll do stuff like palpate the carotid arteries in the neck and the temporal arteries just in front of the ears. Then the wrists. Then the bell of the stethoscope is deployed, low on the forehead, just above the orbits. 'Close your eyes,' says Tod to the patient, who, of course, immediately opens them. 'Take my hand. Raise your left arm. Good. Just relax for a while.' Then it's *talkdown*, which will typically go like this:

Tod: 'It might start a panic.'

Patient: 'Shout *fire*.'

Tod: 'What would you do if you were in a theatre and you saw flames and smoke?'

Patient: 'Sir?'

Tod pauses. 'That's an abnormal response. The normal response would be: "Nobody's perfect, so don't criticize others."'

'They'll break the glass,' says the patient, frowning.

'What is meant by the saying: "People in glass houses shouldn't throw stones"?'

'Uh, seventy-six. Eighty-six.'

'What's ninety-three minus seven?'

'1914-1918.'

'What are the dates of the First World War?'

'OK,' says the patient, sitting up straight.

'I'm now going to ask you some questions.'

'No.'

'Sleeping OK? Any digestive problems?'

'I'll be eighty-one in January.'

'And you're . . . what?'

'I don't feel myself.'

'Well, what seems to be the problem?'

And that's it. They certainly don't look too cheerful on their way out. They back off from me with their eyes wide. And they're gone. Pausing only to do that creepy thing—knocking, quietly, on your door. At least I can say that I do these old guys no real or lasting harm. Unlike nearly all the other patients at AMS, they go out of here in no worse shape than when they came in.

The social standing enjoyed by doctors is of course impressively high. When you move, as a doctor, through society, with your white coat, your black bag, the eyes of others seek you upward. Mothers express it best: their postures seem to say that you have the power over their children; as a doctor, you can leave the children alone, and you can take them away, and you can bring them back, if you choose to. Yes, we walk tall. Us doctors. Our presence chastens others, renders others serious. The tilted eyes of others gives the doctor his smileless nimbus, his burnish of godlike might. And for what? For *this* shit . . . One thing that's helping me through it (and I guess there's an irony here) is that Tod and I are feeling so damn good these days: physically. I can't think why Tod doesn't seem to appreciate the improvement. When I think back to how things were out in Wellport, man, we were still walking, but only just. It was taking us twenty-five minutes to cross the room. We can bend over now with barely a groan, barely a knee-crackle. We're up and down those stairs—Jesus, where's the fire? Occasionally we get bits of our body back, from the trash. A tooth, a toe-nail. Extra hair. And sometimes, and sometimes for hours on end, nothing hurts.

I say that Tod doesn't appreciate the improvement. Well, if he does, he's pretty cool about it, mostly. But there is one thing. As if in celebration—or maybe it's a form of *training*—Tod and I have started doing a sexual thing with our self. Not very enthusiastically, and not at all successfully either, so far as I can ascertain. Tod? I don't know. How is it for you? Any good? Because from my point of view it's a total flop.

I puzzle at the local economy, the commerce, the sad arrangements of the ignored city. And this I get plenty of opportunities to do—to puzzle at it, I mean. I puzzle a lot, if the truth be known. In fact I am forming the impression that I am generally a little slow on the uptake. A real lunk, sometimes. Possibly even subnormal, or mildly autistic. It may very well be that I'm not playing with a full deck. It's certainly the case that I appear to be hitched up with Tod like this, but he's not to know I'm here, and I feel unique and alone, uniquely alone . . . Tod Friendly, stocky, emollient Tod Friendly, moves around freely in the city's substructures, the shelters, the centres, the half-way houses, the flops. He isn't one of the entrenched busybodies or Little Annie Fixits who serenely police these mysterious institutions, where *abuse* is the buzzword. He comes and goes. He suggests and directs and recommends. He's one of grief's middlemen. For life here is junkie, is hooker, is single-parent, is no fixed abode.

Hookers have this thing for mature men. They do. You hardly ever see them bothering with guys their own age. Watchfully the johns back their way into the significant rooms, the little apartments of the low tenement on Herrera, a building which basks in its own brand of dampness and dread. An act of love occurs, for which the john, or the 'trick' as he's called, for some reason, will be quickly reimbursed. I once witnessed such a transaction: the girl took the bills from the crux of her brassière and laid them out among the dresser's rubble; with trembling hands the john then discreetly pocketed his pay. Afterward, the couple will fondly stroll back on to the street, and part. The men slope off, looking ashamed of themselves (doing it for money like that). Ravenously the hooker will remain, on the sidewalk, in tanktop, in hotpants, killing time before her next date. Or hitching rides to nowhere with the additional old stiffs who cruise by in their cunning old cars. Tod is quite often to be found in the tenement of whores. He's a senior citizen, so the girls are forever putting their moves on him. But Tod's not there for the sex and the dough. On the contrary. *He* shells out, and always keeps his pants on. Basically it seems that Tod scores drugs there. The deals are conducted mostly on paper, though sometimes he will take his syringe from the black bag and draw a shot of tetracyclene or methadone from arm or rump. Sometimes too there are physical injuries to be tackled, over there in the tenement on Herrera, with its twisted sheets, its stained bidets.

Half-way houses are places at which people stop by on their way to prison, where they are trained for serious crime (with dumb-bells, boredom, the low grumble of the exercise yard). At the flops, the guys all eat the same thing. Unlike a restaurant or the little cafeteria at AMS. It's not good, I think, when everyone eats the same thing. I know that none of us has any choice about what we eat; but I get a woozy feeling when I watch them spoon away, and the plates—twenty or thirty of them—all fill up with the same thing. Junkies sell blood. The women at the refuges and the crisis centres are all hiding from their redeemers. The crisis centre is not called a crisis centre for nothing. If you want a crisis—just check in. The cuts, the welts, the black eyes get starker, more livid, until it is time for the women to return, in an ecstasy of distress, to the men who will suddenly heal them. Some require more particular treatment. They stagger off and go and lie in a park or a basement or wherever, until men come along and rape them, and then they're OK again.

It's lucky that the city is getting better, and getting better so fast.

I am naturally much buffeted by Tod's responses to these exhausting and unwelcome stimuli. And I have to say that he strikes me as typically perverse and mean-minded in his attitude to the pimps. The pimps—these outstanding individuals, who, moreover, lend such colour to the city scene, with their clownishly customized clothes and cars. I would like to ask Tod the following question. What on earth would become of the poor girls without their pimps, who bankroll them, who *shower* money on them? All right, so the girls blow it all on the old men. So what! Oh, I suppose they'd be better off left to Tod's tender mercies, would they? All *he* does is go round there and rub dirt in their wounds. And gets out quick, before the long-suffering pimp shows up and knocks the chick into shape with his jewelled fists. As he works, the baby in the cot beside the bed will hush its weeping, and sleep peacefully, secure in the knowledge that the pimp is come.

Mothers bring Tod their babies in the night. Tod discourages this—but he's usually pretty sympathetic. The mothers pay him in antibiotics, which often seem to be the cause of the babies' pain. You have to be cruel to be kind. The babies are no better when they leave, patiently raising hell all the way to the door. And the moms crack up completely: they go out of here *wailing*. It's understandable. I understand. I know how people disappear. The little children on the street, they get littler and littler. At some point it is thought necessary to confine them to pushchairs, later to backpacks. Or they are held in the arms and quietly soothed—of course they're sad to be going. In the very last months they cry more than ever. And no longer smile. The mothers then proceed to the hospital. Where else? Two people go into that room, that room with the forceps, the soiled bib. Two go in. But only one comes out. Oh, the poor mothers, you can see how they feel—during the long goodbye, the long goodbye to babies.

RYSZARD KAPUŚCIŃSKI
in

Ryszard Kapuściński, whose 'Bolivia, 1970' appears in this
issue, is a regular contributor to Granta.
His other pieces include:
'Warsaw Diary' in *Granta* 15
'Warsaw Diary Part Two' in *Granta* 16
'A Tour of Angola' in *Granta* 20
'Outline for a book that could have been written' in *Granta* 21
'Christmas Eve in Uganda' in *Granta* 26
'The Snow in Ghana' in *Granta* 28
These issues are now available in bookshops, at £5.99 each.
Or order from Granta, FREEPOST, 2-3 Hanover Yard, Noel
Road, Islington, London N1 8BE.

Please send me the following back
issues, at £5.99.

☐ *Granta* 15

☐ *Granta* 16

☐ *Granta* 20

☐ *Granta* 21

☐ *Granta* 26

☐ *Granta* 28

☐ Three of the above at £15.00
For foreign orders, add £1 for postage
for each issue.

Name _____

_____ Postcode _____

Payment ___ cheque enclosed
___ credit card Access/ American Express/Diners
Club/Visa no. _____
Credit card orders can be accepted by phone (071) 740 0470

Signature _____

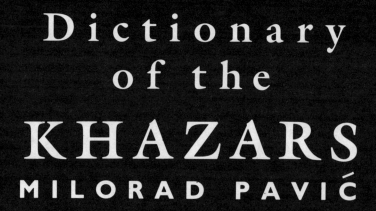

Dictionary of the KHAZARS

MILORAD PAVIĆ

MALE EDITION

One paragraph is crucially different.

THE CHOICE IS YOURS

WATERSTONE'S BOOKSELLERS

SHERRATT & HUGHES

Dictionary
of the
KHAZARS
MILORAD PAVIĆ
FEMALE EDITION

*One paragraph
is crucially
different.*

**THE CHOICE
IS YOURS**

SHERRATT
& HUGHES

Notes on Contributors

William McPherson won the Pulitzer Prize in 1977 for book reviews and literary essays published in the *Washington Post*, where he was a columnist and editor. He is the author of two novels. **Isabel Ellsen** is a photographer and journalist. She lives in Boulogne. **Victoria Tokareva**'s story 'Centre of Gravity' appeared in *Granta* 30. She lives in Moscow and has recently completed a collection of stories. **Hans Magnus Enzensberger** contributed to the symposium 'The State of Europe' in *Granta* 30. A collection of his poems, *The Sinking of the Titanic*, was published in English last year. **Christa Wolf** is a member of the Central Committee of the East German Writers' Union. Her novels include *A Model Childhood, No Place on Earth* and *Cassandra*. She won the National Prize in 1978 and was runner-up for the Nobel Prize in 1988. **Ryszard Kapuściński** was born in 1932 in Pinsk in eastern Poland, a region that is now part of the Soviet Union. Throughout the sixties and seventies he was the sole correspondent of PAP, the Polish Press Agency, covering Africa and, later, Latin America. *The Soccer War*, the autobiography of Kapuściński's Third World travels, will be published by Granta Books in October. **Ferdinando Scianna** lives in Milan. A retrospective of his work, *Le Forme del Caos*, was published in Italy in 1989. **Isabel Allende** lives in California. 'The Judge's Wife' appeared in *Granta* 21. 'Gift for a Sweetheart' will be included in *The Stories of Eva Luna* to be published early next year. **Bill Roorbach** and Juliet Karelsen were married on 23 June. They are in the Loire valley (on honeymoon) as this issue goes to press. His book *Summers with Juliet* will be published by the Houghton Mifflin Company. **Romesh Gunesekera** grew up in Sri Lanka and now lives in London. *Monkfish Moon*, a collection of his stories, will be published by Granta Books in 1991. Martin Amis's most recent novel is *London Fields*. 'Time's Arrow' is the provisional title of a work in progress.

Granta notes with sadness the death of Michael Glenny, 1927–1990, translator of Russian and a great friend of the magazine.